Worship

A heart for God

D1614490

Other books by Bryn Jones:

According to Your Faith (Harvestime)
Effective Prayer (Harvestime)

Worship

A heart for God

Bryn Jones

Harvestime

Published in the United Kingdom by:
Harvestime Services Ltd, 12a North Parade, Bradford
West Yorkshire BD1 3HT
Copyright © 1989 Bryn Jones
First published by Harvestime
First printed August 1989

Scripture quotations are generally taken from the
New International Version.
Copyright © 1978 by the New York
Bible Society and published by Hodder & Stoughton.
Used by permission

Other versions referred to: Revised Authorised Version (RAV),
New American Standard Bible (NASB), King James Version (KJV)

British Library Cataloguing in Publication Data:

Jones, Bryn
  Worship.
  1. Christian church. Worship
  I. Title
  264

ISBN 0-947714-70-7

Typeset in the United Kingdom by:
Emset, London NW10 4EH
Printed and bound in the United Kingdom by:
Richard Clay Ltd., Bungay, Suffolk.

Contents

This book is dedicated to
lovers of God everywhere

Preface

Although worship can be experienced, it can never be adequately explained. Involving both your feelings and understanding, its source is in your spirit.

This is why I haven't attempted to write a definitive study on worship, nor concentrated on the shades of meaning in the relevant Hebrew and Greek words. My desire is to focus attention on the *heart* of worship, to emphasise its essential foundation and spirit.

I haven't written to inform but to provoke, not so much to instruct as to inspire you to worship. Sometimes, I fear, form and technique are in danger of obscuring the simplicity and spontaneity of worship.

Everywhere the cry today is: 'What's your ministry? What role do you play in the church? Are you a leader of a group? What has God called you to?'

How often I have longed to shout, 'Stop! Stop!' It's time we remembered that, of all that we can be or do in the church of God, nothing is of greater value or of higher privilege than being a worshipper, a lover of God.

Bryn Jones
August 1989.

1

Springs of worship

Those who sing as well as those who play the flutes shall say, 'All my springs of joy are in you.'
Psalm 87:7 NASB

John sat straight-backed at the organ, his slender hands moving skilfully across the keyboard, his feet working furiously on the pedals to pump air into the lungs of the tired instrument. Despite squeaks and rushes of air as it raspingly responded to his efforts, the organ did its best, as though not wishing to destroy his confidence.

Meanwhile, the pastor, suitably attired in his Sunday suit, stood erect, hymnbook in hand, to lead in worship the subdued and wearied followers lined up before him.

I remember, on that warm summer morning, rising from the pew that tried to hold me down—my trousers had stuck to the varnished seat with the summer heat!

Leaning on the back of the pew in front like some half-awake Saturday night leftover, I resigned myself to a miserable morning and thought how dreadful it was that the hymn we were singing had so many verses. Most of the lines made no sense to me at all. Even worse, there would be three more hymns like this one before the meeting finished!

To some of the congregation the whole thing may have been an inspiration, but to me it was incredibly boring. I tried my best to inject feeling into that morning's 'worship', but it was like squeezing a shrivelled orange for the last drop of juice, only to be disappointed when nothing comes.

The pastor had told us at the start of the service that we would spend eternity engaged in worship. I couldn't think of a more appalling prospect. Surely that wouldn't be eternal life—more like eternal endurance!

Since then I've changed my mind, partly because I've found some of those songs to contain sublime truths well-expressed, but chiefly because I've discovered and drunk from the springs of joy in worship.

Among all creatures, only man is a worshipper. Churches, temples, synagogues, mosques or shrines—all are symbols of man's desire to worship. Yet we must discover the springs of joy in worship if we are to please him by our worship.

Spiritual worship isn't trying to understand what others meant by the words of hymns they wrote generations ago; it is expressed in what *we* feel in our love for God *today*.

True worship results from the releasing of the inner springs of our spirit in response to a present, living revelation of God. It is through such worship that our spirit reaches upwards to our highest goal—God himself. And in doing so, we find our own deepest longings fulfilled.

Because of the infinite nature of God our worship in eternity will never be tedious, for our revelation of God will not be complete when we receive our redeemed bodies. In the age to come, the wonder of the unfolding of his nature will continually provoke in all his worshipping creatures new songs of praise and adoration.

In this way we will experience progression in our worship. Not one song of praise, shout of glory or confession of worship will ever need to be repeated.

In the meantime, we worship in response to what he reveals of himself now. But in today's world we have become used to living with the imperfect and substandard. The less than ideal is now accepted as the norm. So any sudden disclosure of the moral perfections of God's fulness can be quite overwhelming. Yet nothing excites our human heart so much as a sudden revelation of the divine.

Our worship progresses as it is enriched, expanded and deepened by these self-disclosures of the Almighty. Doors are thrown open within us as we are lifted above the clamour of everyday life into the presence of his peace, where we experience the deepest of pleasure. 'You have made known to me the path of life; you will fill me with joy in your presence, with eternal pleasures at your right hand' (Psalm 16:11).

But God doesn't show himself to the casual believer nor force a revelation of himself upon the unseeking. It is those who search for him with all their hearts who find him at the heart of everything. And just as we are provoked to worship by his presence, so we provoke in him a response to our worship: 'I love those who love me, and those who seek me find me' (Proverbs 8:17).

As Moses walked in the desert with a longing after God, he took his sheep near the mountain of God's presence. Deep inside he felt his heart warming. Suddenly a little bush burst into flame. It was a common thing in the desert for bushes to catch fire. But whereas they were burnt out in a few minutes, this flame burned on.

Moses felt the hair rising on the back of his neck. There was a quickening of his pulse, a stirring of excitement. He said to himself, 'I will go over and see this strange sight—why this bush does not burn' (Exodus 3:3).

Did that statement express a vestige of hope? Did he wonder if, after all these years, God had at last come to him again?

The Bible records, 'When the Lord saw that he had gone over to look, God called to him from within the bush, "Moses! Moses!" ' (v4). Have you ever wondered why God didn't say any more than that at first? God called his name and waited to see how Moses would respond, for *God responds to our responses.*

Sometimes God breaks in on our lives with a 'burning bush' experience—something happens to us that we know is not natural. It has the hallmarks of divine intervention. As a result, we turn aside into the secret place to seek God, and he responds to our response. Our heart fills with worship, praise and love and suddenly we are again in the presence of the Most High.

Once it happened to me when the load began to bear down on me: the telephone calls, correspondence, meetings, people, demands of work and home, travel arrangements, last minute changes, publicity, preparation. All the administrative details involved in itinerant ministry seemed to crowd in on me.

I knew I wasn't the only one thus pressured, so it was pointless holding a private pity-party. The accelerated pace of the movement of God's Spirit had resulted in new and growing churches, which meant an increased after-care ministry.

I have never been a man afraid of work and have engaged in active ministry among people. But that day I was feeling unusually tired, not just physically but mentally and emotionally as well.

In this busy world you can all too easily find yourself swamped with commitments which take from you but don't replenish. You can quickly find yourself burning up your resources to meet the demands of life. I wondered whether I had fallen into this trap.

I asked myself, 'Am I just overworked, or am I a victim of a lack of wisdom on my part? Am I in danger of losing Christ in the busyness of ministry?'

That evening, long after everyone had gone to bed, I sat in the darkened room simply listening to the silence.

I felt too tired to pray. I just closed my eyes before the glow of the open fire, whispering, 'I love you, Lord.' And in saying it again and again I realised that, if everything else had to go, all else be stripped away, this was the deepest longing of my spirit: to love the Lord.

Whatever the activities and tasks of the future age; however involved we become in the restoration of the universe to its true purpose; however deeply engaged we are in the restructuring of this world so that it is to the glory of God and the blessing of humankind; whatever our task in this world or the one to come—our greatest occupation as lovers of God will always be to worship him.

2

Tears turn our 'whys' into worship

Man is not made to question, but to adore.
Edward Young

I watched Joan as she sat by the still form of her husband lying lifeless on the bed, her black hair and smooth, pale skin perfectly matching his own.

The clock ticking in the room seemed to set the metre for her movements as she silently rocked back and forth, stroking his cold hand, while a tear ran down her face.

I looked at their wedding photo in its neat silver frame on the dressing-table, alongside another taken more recently with their two lovely children.

They'd had five beautiful years together, but now he was gone. The faraway look in her eyes said she was reaching into the past and drawing from the shared love stored in the bank of her memory. She desperately needed this support now to go on living, for her two little ones needed her more than ever.

I didn't know what to say or do. Why did he have to go now, I wondered? So soon, so young, so needed, so loved. Why had God allowed it? My feelings and thoughts crashed into each other—anger, pity, love, sorrow. The one word drumming in my mind over and over again was, 'Why? Why? Why?'

I just stood there, helpless but sharing her grief. Then, quietly, as I rested my hand on her shoulder, I heard her whisper, 'Thank you, Lord; thank you, Lord.'

Many harsh, traumatic experiences leave us hurt and confused. Whole episodes of life seem shrouded in mystery. There are times of pain that leave us so drained that there isn't even enough strength left to feel the emotion of anger.

There's the young couple who are buying their first home. They have carefully budgeted their income so that they will not be unduly pressured by mortgage repayments. Suddenly, in a time of economic decline, one or other loses their job. It is a major financial setback threatening their blissful future, causing them to ask, 'Why?'

Or there's the godly parents who have diligently set an example of Christian living for their children to follow. Suddenly, their teenager starts running with a bad crowd and going wrong in life. They puzzle over it, searching themselves for an answer as to why.

Then there's the businessman who for years has ploughed back his profits into building up the business. He and his family have sacrificed for so long to see the business become a success. Now they find themselves wiped out financially within weeks and together they ask, 'Why?'

The 'whys' of life are many, touching us in the deepest areas of our family life, business, dreams, hopes and friendships.

But even when our mind is trapped by the 'why' of it all, our heart can still worship. When Job experienced the sudden, tragic loss of all his children, instead of cursing or denouncing God he embraced the heart-rending hurt in the mystery of God's working by releasing himself in worship: 'At this, Job got up and tore his robe and shaved his head. Then he fell to the ground in worship' (Job 1:20).

If our spirit doesn't absorb the sorrows of life and turn them into worship, we will twist them into something else: bitterness, self-pity, resentment or accusation against God.

16

This is what Paul meant when he said, 'Brothers, we do not want you to be ignorant about those who fall asleep, *or to grieve like the rest of men*, who have no hope' (1 Thessalonians 4:13). We will grieve, but not with the grief of the hopeless.

Through worship we are able to take hold of the issues that reach out to hurt us. By embracing them into the love of God we draw their sting and turn the occasion of potential harm into blessing. In this way we discover that the deepest waters of life flow from the heart in worship.

Among the starving masses of famine-stricken countries, the thousands of prisoners of conscience in many lands, the innocent victims of warring states and the trapped poor of our inner city ghettoes—among this unending army of the dying are millions of triumphant souls who have found in Christ hope in their hopelessness. In a spirit of triumph, they shine in the darkness of social injustice like lighthouses in stormy seas. They have risen above their situation on the wings of worship.

Worship doesn't overflow only in songs, shouting or dancing; it is often expressed in our tears.

When God instructed Moses to make the incense of worship for the tabernacle he told him to include *galbanum* among the fragrant ingredients. This was the sap of the Ferula tree. It was contained within the tree until the trunk was slit with a knife. A little of the brownish-coloured gum would then 'weep' from the cut, forming the shape of a tear-drop. Because of this it became known as 'the weeping tree'.

Many times I have seen people desperately trying to suppress tears, as if it would be shameful to display any emotion.

When I was a boy, someone once said to me, 'Dry your eyes! Big boys don't cry.' Later, of course, it became, 'You're a young man now—and men shouldn't cry.'

Tears in adults have become a sign of weakness—an indication that they aren't quite up to the job, evidence of emotional instability or immaturity. Consequently, to prove their 'maturity' many have carefully cultivated the suppression of their feelings. Yet in doing so they are suffering great personal loss.

Jesus wept at the tomb of Lazarus, moved by love and the sorrow of those around him. He wept over the city of Jerusalem in its rejection of him, feeling deeply the heart's desire of his Father for his people: 'As he approached Jerusalem and saw the city, he wept over it and said, "If you, even you, had only known on this day what would bring you peace—but now it is hidden from your eyes"' (Luke 19:41-42).

No doubt his tears frequently flowed freely as he prayed in the secret place. They were part of his seeking of the fulfilment of his Father's will in the saving of the men and women he loved so much.

Nobody is true to his fellow-humans who has not learnt to weep for those who hurt in life. Such crying is not a sign of immaturity but of humanity.

'During the days of Jesus' life on earth, he offered up prayers and petitions with *loud cries and tears* to the one who could save him from death, and he was heard because of his reverent submission' (Hebrews 5:7).

Mary Magdalene led a sordid life before meeting Jesus. Now, overwhelmed by gratitude for his forgiveness, she unashamedly washed his feet with her tears, just as he had washed away her past with his words of love.

The watching Pharisees were repulsed by her behaviour. To them it was in the worst taste of emotional and religious extremism. It was so unseemly, so undignified. They fully expected Jesus to stop this embarrassing spectacle. Jesus, however, understood Mary's feelings—he knew that here was love worshipping in spirit and in truth (Luke 7:37-50).

Many of us Christians are often moved to tears, not so much by pain or hurt, but through the love and grace of God. If someone were to ask, 'Why are you crying?' we would have to reply, 'I don't know—he's just so wonderful.' Such an answer would no doubt leave completely nonplussed those who don't understand the extravagance of love in worship.

Life is filled with laughter and tears. They are not enemies opposed to each other; they are friends, the two wings of the soul in flight. Both are, at different times, healing medicines to the wounds of the heart. They embrace the full range of human experience—our happiness and our pain. Either one without the other would leave us untrue to ourselves.

There are often tears in the heart that never make it to the eye. To lock up our tears is to drown our happiness so that it can no longer express itself in heartfelt laughter. Let us be ready to worship with tears.

3

Climbing the musical stairway

Music is well said to be the speech of angels.
Carlyle

As I sat back in my chair listening to the music, I felt the love of God wash over me. The violin's haunting melody reached inside me and beckoned my soul to climb its musical stairway to the presence of God.

I was enthralled by the purity of that music. The violinist, like some mysterious angelic visitor, filled the room with a heavenly sound, provoking me to worship God.

There is an incredible power in music to stir the soul of men and women. It holds exciting prospects for our deepest desires to express themselves in creative worship.

'Creative' is, sadly, an example of a word devalued through overuse. There are many such words. I remember my young son coming in once, enthusing with his friends about a frozen custard he had eaten. When I asked what it was like he said, 'Awesome!' I smiled at his misuse of the word.

'Creative' has often been made the excuse for introducing unacceptable practices or passing fads. But what I mean when

I say 'creative worship' is that we should not allow ourselves or our expressions of worship to fossilise into ruts and rituals. We must be committed to positive change and progress in every area of life, including our worship.

In loving God with all our heart, soul, mind and strength, we must not allow ourselves to be trapped by history or tradition. Nor must we foolishly determine that all expressions of our worship or Christian life have to be contemporary, popular or experimental.

What we are declaring in our desire to be creative in worship is that everything, whether it be poetry, songs of praise or musical renditions, must be in a form that adequately expresses our convictions and feelings of love for God *now*.

Creative worship is not sloppy or disorganised. Neither does it allow us to remain bound by the patterns of previous generations. Being creative in worship means being enthusiastic, alert, eager to respond to the present moving of the Spirit upon us.

'It is good to praise the Lord and make music to your name, O Most High, to proclaim your love in the morning and your faithfulness at night, to the music of the ten-stringed lyre and the melody of the harp' (Psalm 92:1-3).

Because love is warm and exuberant, it refuses to settle into the rut of the usual or the predictable. Instead it looks for new ways and fresh directions to express its excitement.

This is seen even under the old covenant in the breadth of worship shown by the people of Israel in their music, dance, songs, incense, sacrifices and feasts. And who would dare say that the new covenant love which we now enjoy is to be more restrained in its ingenuity of expression? On the contrary, our inspiration in worship is increased, because redeeming grace has deepened our love for God.

Worship through words, tears or silence is expanded by the addition of the many musical instruments and musical forms now available. I'm sure David explored different musical styles in praise while he watched his sheep on the hills of Bethlehem. As he worshipped with the accompaniment of his harp, God expanded his vision to embrace the prospect of a vast orchestra that would one day lead Israel in worship.

He could see them in his mind's eye: great processions of people going up to the God-filled temple where, surrounded by fragrant incense and the sound of massed musicians and choirs of priests, they would offer their sacrifices of worship.

If the spiritual person is lifted by the music of worship, the ungodly person is angered by it. King Saul in his most irrational moments of violent anger when troubled by an evil spirit, lashed out at the anointed music of David. The restless, evil heart was provoked by the praise-inspired music of the youthful shepherd-king (see 1 Samuel 18:10-11).

If you are musical, you may well be able to express yourself to God in this language more easily than in words. You can release your feelings of love and adoration, hope and joy in this form, just as others do in prose or poetry, songs or words. Go ahead and play to your heart's content!

I remember on one occasion feeling that I was an intruder in the secret place. I entered the church building and, seeing a light in the main auditorium, quietly opened the door. A young man was playing his guitar and singing softly. Peace and pleasure blended together as his face was uplifted to heaven. He had neither eye nor tongue for any except his God.

I stood in silence, transfixed. My breathing became muted. I dared not mar this moment of worship. It seemed to me that not only was his soul bathed in worship but the auditorium had become a God-filled house of praise, with angels crowded in, wondering at God's redeeming grace.

On another occasion I walked by the lake at a camp and found two musicians whose fingers moved skilfully over guitar strings as they sang the song of the Lord. Two men whose fellowship had blended with the Eternal One, whose spirits had joined those of righteous men made perfect. They needed no earthly temple, cathedral or chapel, for beneath the morning clouds and in the company of unseen hosts they were released in an ecstasy of praise.

Music expresses every mood—the quick, tripping music of

the happy soul, the rich, flowing music of the hymns and psalms. And even where we are not intrinsically musical we can still make a 'joyful noise' to the Lord (Psalm 66:1 KJV)!

A church that believes worship to be a central part of its community life will make financial provision for its development. Churches readily and generously commit huge sums to mission programmes, or even to a single evangelistic campaign. But how much do they spend on the development of worship?

Are they investing in good musical instruments for their musicians? Do the larger churches make provision for the support of a musical director to develop worship in the church and to train its musicians and choir? Or do they see this as unimportant?

Then again, what time and money have they invested in studying the acoustics of the building in which they propose to meet? Many building projects are undertaken without due attention to the acoustic suitability for orchestra, choir or congregational worship.

Finally, do they consider sending the musical director and musicians for refresher courses and seminars in their particular field?

All these things reflect the value we place upon worship.

'Come, let us *sing* for joy to the Lord; let us *shout aloud* to the Rock of our salvation. Let us come before him with *thanksgiving* and extol him with *music* and song' (Psalm 95:1-2).

4

Let praises ring!

Let everything that has breath praise the Lord. Praise the Lord.
Psalm 150:6

I was in a small church in Norfolk, singing Charles Wesley's hymn, 'And can it be, that I should gain an interest in the Saviour's blood?'

As I sang, waves of love and gratitude swept over me for what God had done in my life. When we began the fourth verse I let go with all that was in me:

> 'Long my imprisoned spirit lay
> Fast bound in sin and nature's night;
> Thine eye diffused a quickening ray,
> I woke, the dungeon flamed with light;
> My chains fell off, my heart was free,
> I rose, went forth, and followed thee.'

Suddenly, the lady in front of me turned and said, 'You're not from this church, are you?'

I looked at her, rather surprised. 'No,' I replied. 'I'm a visitor. This is my first Sunday.'

'I thought so,' she retorted. 'We don't sing so loudly in this church.' And with a frozen look she turned again towards the front.

I was being made painfully aware of how out of place I was. This glorious hymn of joyous emancipation was being sung in a very subdued manner by the rest of the congregation. Her implication was that loud, enthusiastic singing lacked propriety in the presence of God.

How relieved I was when, later that day, I read how the angels worship around the throne: '*In a loud voice* they sang: "Worthy is the Lamb, who was slain, to receive power and wealth and wisdom and strength and honour and glory and praise!" ' (Revelation 5:12).

The aged apostle John, while exiled on the island of Patmos without the visible fellowship of other Christians, was caught up in the Spirit to witness heaven holding a parade day. Myriads of worshipping angels surged through the heavens, accompanied by drums and shouts: 'I heard what sounded like a great multitude, like the roar of rushing waters and like loud peals of thunder, shouting: "Hallelujah! For our Lord God Almighty reigns. Let us rejoice and be glad and give him glory!" ' (Revelation 19:6-7).

Heaven was having a holy jamboree!

In responding to God's invitation to cross the threshold of the open door into heaven, John had escaped the confinement of our time-space world. He was no longer locked into the temporal and visible. In spirit he was moving upwards to the eternal Spirit, upwards to the invisible realities of God's presence.

He didn't feel himself an exile; on the contrary, he felt like a son come home. He had found the place of praise. For man is nowhere more fulfilled or more in harmony within himself, never more conscious of his creative destiny than when worshipping his God. Hallelujah!

There is, in fact, no indication that God has any other way for us to come into his presence except through praise: 'Enter his gates with thanksgiving and his courts with praise' (Psalm 100:4).

26

Christian worship is not a solitary experience, for in worship the seen and unseen sides of the universe join hands. As new creatures in Christ we are part of a visible and invisible, social and spiritual complex that unites in worshipping God. In our worship we share with all those worshipping simultaneously on both sides of the veil.

If the heart is filled with praise to God, the mouth surely cannot remain silent. Jesus said, 'The good man brings good things out of the good stored up in his heart, and the evil man brings evil things out of the evil stored up in his heart. For out of the overflow of his heart his mouth speaks' (Luke 6:45).

The heart is the seat of the affections. It is in the heart that every worthwhile quality of life is contained. Charles Swindoll has called it the 'womb of character'.

The God-filled, Christ-centred heart of the believer cannot but overflow in vocal expression of adoration of the Almighty. The Spirit-filled heart will give rise to Spirit-induced worship. It is therefore important that we guard our hearts and what we allow our minds to dwell on (Proverbs 4:23; 23:19).

Israel's feasts and times of sacrifice were loud, boisterous occasions. Equally today, in the new covenant, our sacrifices, while no longer those of bulls and goats, should be filled with joyful expressions of vocal praise overflowing from hearts full of thankfulness and love to God: 'Through Jesus . . . let us continually offer to God a sacrifice of praise—the fruit of lips that confess his name' (Hebrews 13:15).

All that we do in life should be done with enthusiasm. Indeed, God's first and strongest commandment urges us to put everything into serving and worshipping him (Deuteronomy 6:5). If we weep, let the tears flow. If we are happy, let our laughter roll. And if we are to praise our God, let's not only whisper it, but sing his high praises.

I don't mean that we should stride carelessly into the presence of God, or engage in meaningless or empty shouts of praise. Rather, from the fulness of our hearts we should unashamedly declare his wonders and his worth. For then the shouts of our praise will come as whispers in his ear, and the boldness of our entry into his presence will be as the soft tread of the angels.

It is those who have learnt to release their feelings who are the best equipped to serve and help others. People respond when they know they are loved. Our generation has been profoundly affected not just by those with wisdom in a crisis, with the right ideas and political power to initiate change, but by those who have felt deeply, strongly, and who have been able to communicate their feelings compassionately to others.

High praise has rejuvenating power. I remember years ago gathering at the building site with a group of men from the church. We were all feeling tired. It had been a long, hard day. First our own jobs, then the rush home from work, a quick meal and change before gathering on that hot summer evening to dig the footings for the new church building.

We were a mix of strong men and young lads. Though we dug, shovelled and wheelbarrowed until it was too dark to continue, at the end of it, instead of being tired, we had all regained energy: Jack's rich Welsh tenor voice had led us throughout in song and praise to God.

When it was too dark to work we went indoors for a cup of tea. Then, as strong lovers of God, we praised and prayed, shouted and sang together some more.

I turned to Jack. 'It's nearly midnight,' I said. 'I've got to go, but I don't feel tired.'

'No, boyo,' he replied, with a twinkle in his eye. 'When you worship the Lord and wait upon him your strength is renewed. You mount the sky like an eagle. You can run and not be weary, and you can walk and not faint.'

Laughing, we all bade each other farewell and made our way home. But I had discovered something new about worship: when it renews and refreshes the spirit, it also spreads a healing balm upon body, mind and heart.

5

Behold his beauty

One thing I ask of the Lord, this is what I seek: that I may dwell in the house of the Lord all the days of my life, to *gaze upon the beauty* of the Lord and to seek him in his temple.

Psalm 27:4

The three-day convention had been exciting but exhausting.

From morning till night I had been surrounded by people. Many had wanted me to pray with them, some had simply needed a listening ear, others had required counsel. In their different ways they had all drawn from me. But now it had ended and I was on the long drive home.

Rain was lashing down from a dark sky, the windscreen wipers struggling to cope. Although it was only early afternoon, the headlights of oncoming vehicles kept dazzling my eyes. With the traffic bunched together and the road slippery-wet, I had to concentrate on careful driving.

I arrived home mentally and emotionally drained.

Our children were then very young, and I had no sooner been warmly welcomed by my wife and gone into the lounge with a cup of hot tea than the door flew open and in rushed all four of them, home from school. I was caught up in a whirlwind of chatter, laughter and activity as they welcomed me home.

Then, just as children do, they all shot away as suddenly as they had arrived, one to the kitchen, another to his room, the others to play. The room was strangely still again.

At that moment tiredness overwhelmed me and, as I sank into the cushions of 'Dad's chair', my eyelids started to droop. Then, quietly, the door opened and my youngest little girl came in. Without a word, she climbed on to my lap and snuggled down contentedly in my arms. I waited for her to speak but she didn't say anything.

After a while I broke the silence, whispering, 'What do you want, sweetheart?'

'Nothing,' she replied.

'Nothing at all?'

'No, just to sit here with you.'

Suddenly, I felt so warm inside.

Everybody loves to be loved, and how beautiful is the simplicity of love in a child!

The two of us just sat there in the glow of the fire that flickered in the open fireplace. The old clock ticking away was the only sound in the room. We didn't say anything but we were both happy and secure, at home together.

What the convention, with all its demands, had taken out of me, her love was putting back in. She wasn't looking for prayer, for counsel or even for a listening ear—just for me. And though she would have been hard-pressed to articulate her feelings, she was being as much refreshed and warmed by my love as I was by hers.

We were touching something of the emotion which I believe King David experienced in worship—expressed in the psalm quoted at the head of this chapter. He knew that worship is not rushing into God's presence with a thanksgiving-list and an even longer shopping-list of wants, but coming simply to be with him, to love him and to sit quietly in his presence.

David had been an active man, with the demands of a nation pulling on him. Yet now, in this time of silent reflection, all his desires were reduced to 'one thing'. All his energies, all his thoughts, all his feelings were harnessed and concentrated to this single end—an end that would, paradoxically, herald a new beginning.

He realised, much as I did that day, that all his deepest longings would only be satisfied in the secret place of worship before the Lord. Without this experience, whatever else he accomplished could never be fulfilling. Undoubtedly this revelation provoked David's statement, 'As for me, it is good to be near God' (Psalm 73:28).

It is being near him that brings everything else into perspective.

He alone is the measuring-line of our lives. He is the one who gives all other things in life their meaning and without whom nothing in life has real significance. Beholding him widens our intellectual as well as our spiritual horizons. In his presence the eternal outweighs the temporal, the sublime the mundane.

I was once listening to a young man preaching. The intonation of his voice, the way he moved his hands, the smile—all seemed so much like one of my colleagues. I knew my colleague spent more time with this young man than anyone else did.

'Is this an effort to achieve the same response that comes from my colleague's preaching?' I wondered. Then I thought, 'No, it's inevitable, if you spend time with someone, admiring, respecting and watching him closely, that what he is and does rubs off and you absorb much of it into your own personality.'

And so it is when we take time to behold the beauty of the Lord, to gaze upon him. It is here in the place of worship that angels accompany our spirit to a world beyond ourselves, allowing us to see God's character, to learn his secrets, to listen to the depths of his counsels.

All this inevitably rubs off on us. We absorb into our being so much that we have learned at the feet of Christ in worship. What we see is what we become, and in seeing the glory of the Lord we are changed from one degree of glory to another. It is as we look upon him, gazing tenderly and lovingly into his eyes, that we are transformed into his likeness.

Have you thought about how much time you actually devote

to worshipping God? Most of us regularly give time to reading the Bible, praying to God for loved ones, asking for God's blessing, interceding for our world. But how much time is spent quietly in his presence, just to delight in him?

✱ In seeking his face in *prayer* we are saying, 'God, I need you.' But in coming before his presence in *worship,* we are saying, 'God, I love you.'

All true worship is Christocentric because it is in Christ that the history of humankind and the eternity of God meet. In him, human and divine nature are in perfect accord. To men and women Christ is what they would want God to be. Before God, Christ is what God intends man to be. That is why we rejoice with Paul in the revelation that we are 'in Christ', for we worship him who is the perfection we ourselves are becoming (see 2 Corinthians 3:18).

Jesus Christ is the guarantee of the success of God's ultimate purpose. In seeing him we are looking towards the final transfiguration of the whole created order: of humankind first, and then, through men and women, the liberation of the rest of creation. We cannot help falling silent before such a prospect embodied in his person.

Our worship-times of love-filled silence are both a delight to the Lord and of deep benefit to the soul of the worshipper. They provide the seasons in which, emotionally and mentally, we are restored and enriched. All strain disappears as our hearts and minds are filled with the beauty of the Lord.

Isaiah knew what it meant to be strengthened as he waited in the presence of the Lord: 'He gives power to the weak, and to those who have no might he increases strength. Even the youths shall faint and be weary, and the young men shall utterly fall, but those who *wait on the Lord* shall renew their strength; they shall mount up with wings like eagles, they shall run and not be weary, they shall walk and not faint' (Isaiah 40:29-31 RAV).

Worship will always have its seasons of high praise, great joy and expressive excitement. But some of its deepest and most enriching moments are those when you can truly say to the

32

Lord, 'I just want to be with you,' and quietly you sit, kneel or lie in silence, your heart filled with his love.

It may be that life has robbed you—taken so much out of you and left you feeling cold and rejected. In a drab, colourless, winter world without song, your soul remains empty, dry, wrinkled and forgotten.

But just as the sun and showers of spring will cause everything to come to life again after winter, so your life can know the freshness of springtime in his presence. In the same way as the grass recovers its greenness and the countryside is reclothed in splendid colour, blossoming once more in flowering array, so you, too, as you wait on him, will experience a restoring and refreshing of your soul.

6

Creation sings

The aim of life is to live, and to live means to be aware, joyously, drunkenly, serenely, divinely aware.

Henry Miller

The day I became a Christian I remember walking outdoors and suddenly becoming aware of the wonder of life around me.

I noticed the greenness of the mountain that rose above our house, the colour of the flowers along the pathway. I could hear the birds singing in the hedgerows all around me.

'What's happened?' I thought. 'Why is everything so alive?'

Then I realised. It wasn't the mountain, the flowers or the birds, but me. *I* had changed! I'd been born again and this was the first day of my new life. Everything was wearing its best clothes and singing its finest songs to welcome me into God's kingdom.

'If anyone is in Christ, he is a new creation; the old has gone, the new has come!' they seemed to sing.

I started to whistle a tune and walk with a spring in my step. Every day since then, for the past thirty-four years, I have felt most at one with creation when praising God.

Who has not marvelled at the beauty of a bird in flight, the colour of an opening flower, the green grass on the hill? Listening to the tumbling waters of a mountain stream, how can anyone remain unmoved among creation's splendour?

Creation is its own cathedral, with the sky as its roof and the sounds of life filling the air. The trees, the birds, the wind and the streams provide the accompanying symphony to our worshipping hearts.

Everything God created has the ability and capacity to evoke eternal praise. 'Praise the Lord. Praise the Lord from the heavens, praise him in the heights above . . . . Praise the Lord from the earth . . . . Let them praise the name of the Lord, for his name alone is exalted; his splendour is above the earth and the heavens' (Psalm 148:1, 7, 13).

The eagle climbing the sky, the breaking of ocean waves on the rocks, the sound of the wind in the trees—all remind us that not only men and women but all creation is straining to release its song of praise.

'The creation waits in eager expectation for the sons of God to be revealed' (Romans 8:19). What new song will fill the universe when redeemed people and redeemed creation jointly express their worship to the King of kings!

Recently I drove through some of the loveliest parts of Scotland. The grey clouds made the tall mountains loom forebodingly over me like some stern schoolmaster, casting dark shadows over the heather-carpeted hillside. Yet how quickly they changed in the sunshine to splendid, grand, smiling figures clothed in garments of green, brown, purple, red, white and yellow.

I looked down beautiful glens where hedgerows, like lace-embroidered hemlines, neatly divided the fields. The sparkling waters of white-flowing rivers wove among the trees and on through fields dotted with contented animals.

The sheer beauty of the scene took my breath away. I wanted to lift my conductor's baton and call on mountains and hills, glens and rivers, streams and trees to join together in a great symphony of praise.

I think I understand the feelings of Isaiah as he prophesied the joyful uniting in worship of God's redeemed people and creation: 'You will go out in joy and be led forth in peace; the mountains and hills will burst into song before you, and all the trees of the field will clap their hands' (Isaiah 55:12).

All lovers of God understand the heart of David, who composed so many of his psalms on the hills of Bethlehem, while the clouds danced across the sky as earth's creation provided the music and song. From the hills he sang out to God's glorious creation to join him in praising God.

'Shout for joy to the Lord, all the earth, burst into jubilant song with music; make music to the Lord with the harp, with the harp and the sound of singing, with trumpets and the blast of the ram's horn—shout for joy before the Lord, the King. Let the sea resound, and everything in it, the world, and all who live in it. Let the rivers clap their hands, let the mountains sing together for joy' (Psalm 98:4-8).

But no aspect of God's creation is more varied than humanity. One day, as I looked across the congregation, I realised what a mixture we were: the loud extrovert, the quiet introvert, the intense and the relaxed, the timid and the bold. I couldn't help wondering which of us made the best worshippers of God.

Then I remembered. Just as the Son of Man came to seek and save those who are lost, searching for them diligently, the Father is diligently seeking worshippers who, regardless of personality, praise without fear and love with abandonment. He wants those whose worship is genuine and released by the Spirit, unaffected by religious ritual and the leaven of hypocrisy.

'A time is coming and has now come,' Jesus said, 'when the true worshippers will worship the Father in spirit and truth, for they are *the kind of worshippers the Father seeks*' (John 4:23).

Everything within us longs to confess our love and adoration of God who, though beyond our comprehension in his ways and his actions, nevertheless orders everything for our blessing and highest good.

So let us worship him. But in doing so we must not limit our concept of worship to our own individual expressions of praise, nor indeed to the corporate gatherings of God's people.

37

Worship can be an act on the part of the *whole universe,* seen and unseen.

In choosing to approach the throne of God, we join the invisible multitudes of angelic beings, the host of believers on earth—and all creation.

I am privileged to work with a group of men who love God and who serve him joyfully together. Some of our most blessed times together have been when we have gone in spiritual retreat to spend time in prayer and worship. At such times God has broken in on us again and again, directing our paths, confirming our direction and quickening us for the task.

Much as I have enjoyed this and drawn great delight from it, there are still those times when I deliberately drive out into the country, up into hills, and walk alone. I love to stand on the mountain-top and let the keen wind blow in my face. I look up to the heavens and praise my God. I look down the valleys and marvel at his creation.

I feel at one with God and his universe and praise him from a love-filled heart.

7

Angelic worship

Praise the Lord. Praise the Lord from the heavens, praise him in the heights above. Praise him, all his angels, praise him, all his heavenly hosts.
Psalm 148:1-2

My mother is one of the loveliest women in the world. In our childhood her sacrifices, love and patience in spite of great hardship produced in us the greatest love and admiration.

One of her little ways of keeping the three of us boisterous children in line was to warn us gently that unless we behaved ourselves we would never get our angel-wings when we got to heaven. I'm sure her heart was sounder than her theology, but her simple faith in angels quietly implanted itself in me.

There is nothing in Scripture to suggest that the worshipping angels started to praise only when God began to work on behalf of mankind. Indeed, as God called the universe into being, each act of God's creative power, as it revealed the diversity and richness of his nature, provoked new outbursts of song and shouting from the angelic companies: 'The morning stars sang together and all the angels shouted for joy' (Job 38:7).

If this first natural creation caused such ecstatic praise and joy, then what shouts of acclamation, waves of adoration and worship will break forth in the future age when angelic beings and redeemed men and women together share the wonder of his new creative acts and works!

I recall an incident in my early days as a Christian which underlined for me the central role angels play in worship before the throne. There was no bus service in our town on Sundays, which for me meant a two-mile walk to the building where we gathered for fellowship. During the walk there was plenty of time to think, which as a rule I welcomed.

Unusually for me, on this particular day I felt downcast. Work wasn't going well, at home I was experiencing difficulties and none of my plans seemed to be working out. The more I considered my situation, the more downcast I became.

On entering the church building I saw Walter, a man whom I had come to admire for his boldness and enthusiasm in praise and testimony. He stood in a shaft of sunlight, his white hair glinting in the sun, his strong, clear face etched with the characteristic lines of so many hard-working miners. His lips were moving soundlessly, tears running down his cheeks.

Quietly, I took my place alongside him, feeling as though I was on holy ground as I slowly lifted my hands.

Suddenly, it was as if heaven opened a door, and in my spirit I heard a voice say, 'Come up here and see . . . .'

Every thought slipped away and I was in the presence of the King. I was aware of the vastness of the heavens and the innumerable companies of angelic beings.

As I stood before the throne of grace I saw the sweeping movements of angelic messengers across the earth as some came in and others moved out. I didn't feel like a stranger. My spirit was at home in the wave upon wave of adoration and worship. My whole being joined with those who cried, 'Holy, holy, holy' (Isaiah 6:3).

At that moment my spirit was fulfilled in a way that nothing else has fulfilled me before or since. My problems melted away in the fire of his glory. My entry before God's presence bathed me in a fresh anointing of his Spirit. Jesus filled my mind in a way I cannot describe.

It was more an overwhelming awareness of his presence than a vision of his person. I was conscious of God filling everything. I had come to 'the spirits of righteous men made perfect', to 'thousands upon thousands of angels in joyful assembly'. I was standing in 'Mount Zion . . . the city of the living God' (Hebrews 12:22).

There was no clash in the multitude of voices, no discord in the diversity of adoration, but instead a beautiful harmony in the music of the spirit. Here, above the tarnishing elements of an age adrift from God, my spirit experienced a new sense of wholeness, for now I was able to 'worship the Lord in the beauty of holiness' (Psalm 29:2 RAV).

I knew this was where I belonged. Here I was received, loved, understood and responded to. I was home.

Everything about worship in heaven is filled with movement, beauty, colour and purpose, just as in creation God has filled his world with a rich variety of plants, trees, fruit, fish, birds, animals and—not least—people.

God urges men and women, boys and girls, to join in the cosmic jubilation. He calls us to stop being so distant and detached, and to allow ourselves to feel—and to express what we feel. He wants us to allow our spirit to be released. When that happens, our whole being will be refreshed and renewed in his presence.

In a time of national distress and personal pain, Isaiah went into the temple to seek the Lord. The vision he received of the Lord as supreme ruler of the heavens gives us an inspiring glimpse of worshipping seraphim. Isaiah saw these mysterious angelic beings in continuous movement around the throne (see Isaiah 6).

The word seraphim means 'burning ones'—an apt name for beings so near to the fiery glory of the ultimate splendour. Oblivious of any onlookers, they engage in adoring declarations of God's worth and beauty, calling provocatively to each other, 'Holy, holy, holy is the Lord Almighty; the whole earth is full of his glory' (Isaiah 6:3).

Something of their ecstasy can be felt by those who know

what it is to stand before the presence of God's throne.

Some would maintain that worship is unrealistic in the midst of all the crisis, dilemma, pain and suffering across the earth. Indeed, they argue, it is the time for intercession and prayer rather than worship. But Isaiah as he stood in the temple in the hour of crisis understood that true worshippers are not snared by the apparent catastrophes of time. Believing that he is *Lord,* they see a divine wisdom at work in the shifting patterns of history; they know that his glory fills the earth.

How often the angels must have peered into the mystery of God's love and wondered at the wisdom that caused fallen man to be redeemed from the prison of self-destruction, making him worthy to stand in the highest presence.

Nowhere is man more attuned to his destiny than when joyfully approaching the throne along the path of worship. On every side he is accompanied not only by the angels but also by those of like mind, heart and spirit, for God is home for the spirit of redeemed man.

Men and women are framed for an existence in which every faculty of their being is engaged and employed in the adoration and service of God. And they are truly fulfilled because in such activity they are most at one with their destiny.

The angels who join us in worship are the ones who also watch over us. The Bible is filled with accounts of angelic activity in furthering the purpose of God and ministering to the needs of men and women. If the veil between the visible and invisible were removed, and we were to see the invisible angels as clearly as we do the material things around us, what a surprise we would have. We would see how often they have been the providers of our needs, the changers of our circumstances, the means by which God has protected us without our being aware of it.

Angels have warded off the powers of darkness that have sought to assault us. They have cleared our pathway in life, removing obstacles. They have lifted our pressures and urged us on. Servants of God they may be, but equally they are sent to be ministers to us, the heirs of salvation.

It was the angels who accompanied Jesus' coming to earth as a baby in Bethlehem. They watched over him as a child, as indeed Jesus said the angels do with all children. It was the angels who strengthened him in the temptation in the wilderness. They ministered to him in the Garden of Gethsemane. They appeared at his resurrection. They announced his return even while he was leaving at his ascension.

All through the ministry of Christ's life the angels were there. And as it was true of him, so it is true of us. God's angels are constantly ministering to us. And how delighted they are when we break forth in worship, for here they, too, are at home and join us in adoration of the King.

8

Worshipping together

I rejoiced with those who said to me, 'Let us go to the house of the Lord.'
Psalm 122:1

We'd been living in the countryside for three years, surrounded by beautiful hills and fields.

It didn't matter what season of the year it happened to be, everything spoke of the beauty of God. The winter snows that covered the hedges and fields, the spring blossom in the orchards, the lamb-filled fields, bright summer days so warm and colourful, the autumn with the changing leaves falling from the trees. Everything was beautiful.

But now suddenly it was all change. We had received an invitation to move to the city and, having prayed about it, we were convinced this was God's will. Finance had been forthcoming, a home was duly purchased and we moved.

We had responded to the invitation to pastor the local church, but quickly found the meetings to be lifeless and deadly quiet. There seemed to be no song of praise among the people.

I decided that I would give a series of several weeks' teaching on worship, for I longed for them to become a praising people.

And so I taught on worship week after week. But at the end of the series, although the people had listened intently, some diligently taking notes, the end result showed no change: the same lifeless meetings.

In my disappointment and frustration I determined to give time to praying to discover why this was so. I busied myself explaining to God the predicament I was in, the difficult nature of this church, the problem of their lifelessness as a people—all the things that, in our moments of foolishness, we think we have to explain to the One who already knows everything better than we can ever explain it anyway!

I said, 'Lord, what can I do?'

'Worship,' replied that inner voice.

'Yes, but they don't seem to know how to worship, Lord. I've explained worship, I've taught worship, but they still aren't worshipping. What else can I do, Lord?'

Again the voice said, 'Worship.'

'But Lord, they're just not worshipping!'

'I didn't say *them,* I said *you* worship.'

That made me think. I had been so busy trying to teach them how to worship, get them to worship, release them into worship that I myself hadn't been worshipping at all.

The following Sunday I sat in the front of the auditorium and quietly began to sing my praise to God. As my spirit flowed in joyous praise, I became momentarily aware of the embarrassing silence all around me. I quickly dismissed it from my mind and went on worshipping until I felt fulfilled in myself. Then I rose, announced my text and began to preach the Word.

The people looked astonished—they had assumed that my purpose in standing would be to introduce a worshipful hymn. Later, as they all quietly filed out, nobody said a word, but I could sense the puzzled questioning in every mind.

During the week I again turned to the Lord: 'Father, there was only me worshipping. What about next Sunday?'

'Worship.'

Sunday came. I went in and did the same. Again I was

surrounded by embarrassed silence, but I went on worshipping, praising and loving God until I lost awareness of the fact that they weren't involved.

Once more I got up to open the Word and preach. Again they all filed out in silence, but it was clear now that they were considering what they should do. Should someone mention things to me, ask what was going on? But I didn't invite any such questioning. At the close of the meeting I simply shook hands and shared pleasantries with them as they left.

The following week I again sat in the front and started to worship. 'Bless the Lord, O my soul, and all that is within me bless his name,' I sang. Suddenly I heard another voice echo mine with, 'Praise ye the Lord.'

As I continued to worship, two or three voices began to join in. Over the next few weeks more and more joined in until, after a couple of months, everyone was free in their praise and expressions of thanks and love for God. We were worshipping!

Spontaneity in public is understandably difficult at first. The watchword of our cold, indifferent and increasingly isolationist neighbourhoods is privacy. People today are anxious to come home from their offices and work-places, shut the door and leave the street deserted as they settle down to their private existence.

In my childhood it was different. Our street had a terrace of forty-two houses on one side and forty houses and a pub on the other. It was always humming with activity. Children would play games while, on quiet evenings, the adults would stand at the doorways talking to neighbours. If it was sunny, many would bring their chairs just outside the door into the street and chat with others.

But all that has gone in the clamour for privacy. People have made their home their prison. The only sign of their presence is the dim light behind the curtains to say someone is in the house. We need to rediscover our social togetherness.

John Donne, a seventeenth century sage, wrote: 'No man is an island, entire of itself, every man is a piece of the continent, a part of the main. If a clod be washed away by the sea, Europe is the less . . . any man's death diminishes me because I am involved in mankind and therefore never send to know for whom the bell tolls, it tolls for thee.'

Many people feel that all worship is so intensely personal that it is best done privately. When they meet together they would rather leave spontaneous, audible worship to the few with extrovert tendencies. Yet one of life's greatest delights is the experience of worshipping God ecstatically together, learning to release our hearts to God in a way that brings down his presence among us.

Such worship often opens the door to the supernatural. Miracles and healings, blessing and salvation are constantly seen among a church who worship freely. The grace of God extends itself to all from within the sanctuary of praise and worship.

Worship is like a river—it flows. It is not a stagnant pool but a flowing experience. As you pour your heart into the river of praise and worship, so others are provoked to do the same until, from all together, there swells a fragrant song of love to God from the hearts of his people.

'Together' is a beautiful word, one that focuses the yearning of humankind. It was never God's intention for people to be alone. We were created as social creatures and it is impossible to be both an isolationist and a fulfilled person.

Throughout its chapters, the book of Acts emphasises the 'togetherness' of fellowship in the early church. They moved from house to house, sharing meals and praying together. They cared for each other, ensuring that the needy were well looked after. They embraced persecution with gladness and faith. They simply enjoyed each other, the contagious joy of their shared life being like a cool breeze in the arid desert of their day.

Some years ago, when inflation and economic recession were affecting the home and family life of thousands of ordinary people, one lady came to the church in deep concern about her situation. She was not a Christian but felt intensely the financial pressures which were causing strain in her marriage.

Raising her voice, she said, 'It's all right for you; you Christians have each other. The rest of us are left to see to ourselves.'

In that moment of perception she touched the heart of the gospel message: we have *each other*. The worshipping experience is not that of a congregation of individuals but the togetherness of a family.

Again and again, while worshipping together, we have experienced the visitation of God, filling us afresh with his power and glory. Each visitation in turn has created a new wave of God-filled worship, God-filled movement, God-filled action, God-filled praise. Everything else has dropped away and God has become the centre of our fellowship together.

> My goal is God himself, not joy, nor peace,
> Nor even blessing, but himself, my God:
> 'Tis his to lead me there, not mine, but his -
> 'At any cost, dear Lord, by any road!'
> *F. Brook.*

9

More than Adam lost

Jesus reigns adored by angels,
Man with God is on the throne;
Mighty Lord, in thine ascension,
We by faith behold our own.

Christopher Wordsworth

I stood on the touchline, hoping I would be chosen to play for my school. I loved the hot, physical game of Rugby football and had been training hard, hoping to be included in the school team. But Gareth was better at scrum-half than I was, so until now my chance had never come.

As the season had progressed, many besides me had seen Gareth's performance slipping. It was clear he had lost form and now the school selectors were considering changes.

Suddenly, I heard my name. I felt great! I was walking on air. I'd been chosen to play scrum-half!

As I looked at Gareth, I saw his face darken. He was angry with me, as though I were to blame for his not being chosen. For the rest of that season he did everything he could to beat me into the mud at games practice. He changed character completely and seemed willing to stoop to any foul that would enable him to win. At times I felt he was deliberately trying to injure me.

None of this escaped the notice of the team trainer, who finally dropped Gareth from reserve position, keeping me on the team for another full season.

People who lose position in life often resent those who take their place. Even though they may have lost it because of their own failings, they tend to shift the blame and take it out on those who fill their former position.

That's how it is with the devil, who hates hearing us give praise and worship to God.

Long before God created humankind, or this world as we know it, he created the angelic orders. There is an intriguing biblical suggestion that those angels were led in worship by Lucifer, a superb musician and choir director: 'You were anointed as a guardian cherub, for so I ordained you. You were on the holy mount of God; you walked among the fiery stones' (Ezekiel 28:14).

Lucifer had a privileged position near the throne. With outspread wings he conducted angelic worship until expelled from God's presence for his proud and rebellious heart.

Having experienced the pleasure and power of worship more than any other creature, the devil has become envious of the privileges enjoyed by redeemed men and women and is filled with bitter memories of the position and joys he has lost.

After Satan fell (Isaiah 14:11-15), Adam came crashing down, too, and the fountain of praise from his once-innocent lips was stopped. A blight fell upon his sinful progeny: man's capacity for praise and worship was decimated. But man's fall has not changed God's creative purpose for him—whose chief end is to glorify and enjoy God for ever.

God has stepped into millions of lives bent on self-destruction and changed their grief and hurt to praise.

One such was Alan. I had just closed the Sunday morning meeting and the musicians were putting their instruments away when suddenly this young teenager bounded up to the platform. He threw his arms around me, held me tightly and sobbed and sobbed. I didn't quite know what to do other than hold him and let him cry.

After a few minutes I looked at young Alan and said, 'What is it, son?'

He began to pour out to me the hurt, the rows that had gone on between his mum and dad and the deteriorating home situation until finally, that week, his dad had left. He didn't know where his dad had gone, and he didn't know if he was ever coming back.

Looking at me, Alan reminded me, 'You said today that God is a God of love. You said God loves us and wants us to be happy and blessed. You said that God would give us our longings. I want my dad to come back home.'

'Alan,' I replied, 'let's ask God together for that, and I promise that if you trust him you won't be disappointed.'

We knelt together by the chair on the platform and as I put my arm around him he began to pray a tearful prayer.

Finally, when he had finished, I remained for a few minutes with my arm around his shoulders and we thanked, praised and worshipped God. There is a wonderful liberation of the soul in worship.

Ten or twelve days later I got a phone call from young Alan to say his dad was home and they were all coming to the church meeting. That Sunday they stood in the meeting, Alan radiant, mum and dad looking sheepish but still managing to give me a smile.

As I closed the meeting in prayer the whole family walked forward. I went down to speak with them and had the joy of leading the father to Christ. Together we worshipped.

Redeemed men and women all over the world enjoy more in Christ than Adam ever lost. For in Christ we have risen higher than Adam ever was, and praise before the throne is now our permanent privilege. As Isaac Watts so aptly expressed it:

> In Christ the tribes of Adam boast
> More blessings than their father lost.

More blessings in the sense that Adam was the earthly man whereas we are of heaven (1 Corinthians 15:47-48). Adam was confined to earth in his rule—we are seated in heavenly places in Christ. Adam had a walk and talk with God each evening in Eden—we are indwelt by God and our fellowship never ceases. It's all day, every day!

To Adam, God was always outside. Much as he enjoyed God's presence and felt the compatibility of his nature with God's, his was never the joy of the redeemed.

We have a song to sing of mercy and grace that has brought us from a condition lower than that in which Adam was created and given us a place higher than Adam ever experienced. Ours is the privilege of being at home in heaven and on earth. In the Spirit we have access to the highest heavens at any time, and we have the privilege of enjoying God on earth in any situation, at any moment, because he dwells within.

What would dare stop us going on to experience the fulness of such blessing, exploring the extent of its possibilities, breaking into new realms of its power? This is what God wants for all of us—that we progress in our union with him.

Nothing will enable us to do that more effectively than preparing ourselves through worship for the working of his Holy Spirit. Closing in with God in wonder, love and praise where he can at any time speak, direct and move. Climbing beyond Adam's best to limitless dimensions of praise and worship—here and now.

10

A thankful heart

This is a sane, wholesome, practical, working faith: first, that it is man's business to do the will of God; second, that God takes on himself the special care of that man; and third, that therefore that man ought never to be afraid of anything.

George MacDonald

The wedding service was over. Both of us, fresh in the joy of our union, were hustled into the car to be taken to the reception. I looked at my bride and again thought how beautiful she was.

When we arrived at the restaurant all the guests crowded in, my wife and I at the head of the table. We sat there, enjoying the meal and the atmosphere, with everyone around us laughing happily. The wedding toasts were being made and the speeches going on when suddenly it hit me.

'Gosh,' I thought, 'the tickets!'

In looking after all the wedding arrangements the one thing I had forgotten to do was buy the train tickets for our journey to the south of England, where we were going on honeymoon!

I put my hands in my pockets and quickly felt around. I only had sixpence. And so it came about that the first question I ever asked my wife was, 'How much money do you have?'

'Nothing,' she replied. 'Why?'

'Oh, never mind, it's okay. Everything's fine.'

I began to perspire. 'O Lord,' I thought, 'what's going to happen when the people discover at the railway station what I've forgotten to do? I'm going to have to embarrassingly confess that I don't have any tickets.'

At that moment a scripture rose to my mind: 'You will know that I am the Lord, for they shall not be ashamed who wait for me' (Isaiah 49:23 RAV).

As the wedding speeches continued I quietly whispered, 'Lord, I believe you. You won't put us to shame. You won't let us be disappointed.' I had no idea how God would do it but I felt the quietness and confidence that he would meet the need.

Then the wedding reception was over. We were bustled off to the hotel room to change and from there into the cars that made a noisy procession down to the railway station.

Just as we turned into Liverpool's Lime Street station, a young man came running along shouting, 'Bryn, Bryn, just a moment. These cards arrived late at the church for you.'

I hadn't even got out of the taxi. I thanked him, took them and started opening them. By the time I had opened the last one I not only had enough money in cash to pay the train fare but we had considerably more left over with which to enjoy the honeymoon.

How good God is! How detailed his care for his children! My heart there and then filled with worship.

It is often by these demonstrations of kindness that God fills our hearts with praise and worship. He does not need lengthy explanations of our needs and difficulties—he simply wants us to thank and worship him in anticipation for his diligent and detailed care for us. And when we receive it, our praise is doubled and tripled.

In 1961 Bob Heslop and I, who had gone through college together, set out for Cornwall—two young evangelists with a single intention: to carry the gospel of Christ through the small villages of South-West England.

We did not know anyone there and, heavily cast on God, looked day by day for our direction from him. We lived in a small caravan belonging to a local greengrocer, from which we set out each day on a visitation programme of the area. Over the next few months we spoke to hundreds of people about Christ.

Our finance was quickly spent in travelling, site fees and food. We were helped with food by daily collecting mushrooms in the fields for breakfast. The only problem was that, after searching for mushrooms day after day, every time I closed my eyes to pray I kept seeing little white blobs rise up in front of me. I knew it was time to change diet or I would end up worshipping the mushroom instead of the Lord!

The inevitable moment arrived when there was no food or money left, and the two of us quietly turned our hearts to God in prayer, calling upon him to provide our need.

Late one evening I went alone across the clifftops at Newquay, wrestling in my mind with our predicament. I imagined headlines springing up in the newspapers: 'Young evangelists starve to death in Cornwall' or 'Religious fanatics die of starvation'. I thought of the terrible shame it would bring on the testimony of God.

As I walked that clifftop I found myself playing with the one penny that was left in my pocket, twisting it between my fingers, turning it over in my hand. I held it as though it were a piece of gold—it was the only money I had in this world.

Suddenly, I felt a surge of exhilaration. I thought, 'God is wonderful, God is good, God is great. He isn't restricted in his ability to meet our needs. Those who trust him will never be disappointed. He has infinite wealth in his treasuries, he owns the cattle on a thousand hills. His Word assures us that, if we are generous, he will supply all our needs according to his riches in glory by Christ Jesus.'

With that I pulled the penny from my pocket, gave it one last look and, laughing, threw it as far as I could from the clifftop out into the sea. As it went I shouted, 'There, devil, I have God's resources at my disposal!'

With that I felt the release of joyous faith and I started to worship and praise the Lord. I think if anyone passing by at that time had noticed me they would have wondered about my mental condition! I went back to the caravan filled with the joy of God.

As I approached the door I noticed a big sack there and thought Bob must have been clearing out old papers or rubbish. Going in, I asked, 'What have you got in the sack outside?'

'What sack?' he said.

Suddenly I realised the sack hadn't been put there by Bob. I quickly went outside. I tried to lift it but it was incredibly heavy, so I called to Bob and together we lifted it indoors. It was filled with tinned foods, a bag of potatoes, two dozen eggs and fruit!

You might say, 'What a wonderful gift pack from someone.' But I knew it was from God, our source, and that the anonymous donor had simply been his means of blessing.

That night Bob and I sat together worshipping and praising the God of supply, the God of care, the God of kindness who will never see us disappointed. There is no need to hold on to the little when we have the God of so much.

How like him to care for us in this way. He provokes us to worship by showing himself to be the God of everyday affairs. We are so often aware of his greatness, majesty and power that we can forget his loving concern for the details of life.

The thankful heart is provoked not simply by the majestic workings of God on a grand scale but also by his everyday kindness in meeting us right where we are.

Have you noticed in the gospels what I can only call the 'quiet miracles', where Christ acted on behalf of the ordinary person, or did something small in itself yet significant to the individual concerned? Once he went with Peter to his home to dine. He was concerned to find that Peter's mother-in-law was ill, and so he performed the miracle of her healing before going on to enjoy fellowship with his disciples. That was one of his quiet miracles, a little thing that he didn't overlook.

Again, as he healed the forgotten people of life, he often whispered to them, 'Don't tell anyone about it,' as though he longed to give to all without craving anything in return.

How like our God, who gives because he loves, not because of what he can get. For what could we give him that is an adequate recompense for what we have received? He gives because he's a giver, he loves because he's a lover, and we love him because he first loved us.

11

A heart aflame

Only passions, great passions, can elevate the soul to great things.
Denis Diderot

No-one will achieve anything unless his heart is passionate in the pursuit of it. I have often been saddened at the dispassionate way in which some people pursue their worship. Worship is meant to be hot, alive, burning, the irrepressible love of a heart aflame.

I remember as a child, while staying with my grandmother, going out among the grass and trees and lighting my little camp-fire. Within minutes I was running back to the house terrified, shouting, 'Gran, Gran, there's a fire!'

What minutes before had been a small flame had leapt upwards, setting fire to the leaves of the trees. Now the tall grass and small trees were ablaze. It took the efforts of the neighbours from all around, as well as the fire brigade, to finally put it out.

How like the spirit of man which, set alight by the love of God, leaps instantly upwards, its flame longing to join the fire that surrounds his throne.

But seeing his eyes like 'flames of fire', we quickly feel our humanity to be so unfitted for the presence of his divinity. Yet it is he who brought us to this place of his presence. He doesn't drive us away. Instead, our experience becomes that of Isaiah, who, feeling so small, unsuited and unclean in the presence of God's burning majesty, was touched by the coals of fire from the altar.

That fire burns up what is unworthy, unacceptable and undesirable in our lives. It continues to burn among the coals on the altars of our hearts as we find a zeal for God, a passion to do his will for his pleasure.

No-one is fitted to be a true servant of God unless the fire of God's love burns in his heart. The Bible teaches us that he makes his servants flames of fire (Hebrews 1:7). It is this burning zeal and passion that causes us to drop all else in our pursuit of the purpose of God for our time. And nowhere does this inner fire of the soul find better fuel than in the time of worship and adoration before his throne.

It was as he emerged from waiting on God in the secret place that the Scripture records of Christ, 'his countenance was changed'. If it was true for him is it not equally true for us? We cannot be in his presence alone for long without experiencing a change in our being. It is impossible to be with him and not be warmed by his presence.

The two lone disciples sharing the pain of his recent crucifixion while trudging along the Emmaus road were startled by the stranger coming alongside. His questions and his words of wisdom burned into their innermost being. Then, as he broke bread with them that evening, they knew it was the Lord. Their description of that experience illustrates the effect of his presence and words in our own lives: 'Were not our hearts *burning within us* while he talked with us on the road?' (Luke 24:32).

Much has been spoken and written about the Christ of the broken heart. Much also should be made of the Christ of the *burning* heart. The zeal with which he pursued the will of God. The anger he displayed at the hypocrisy of the religionists of his day. The convictions he held so immovably. The commitment he displayed towards the disciples. None of it would have been possible had not the flame of God burned strongly within him. As he was, so must we be.

'Ah, but'—those twins of unbelief—now say, 'If you only knew my pressures. I can't stay fervently in love with God all the time.'

But the fire *can* be kept burning. From childhood, one of my delights has been to keep an open fire burning in the home. I have learnt how to bank up the fire on cold winter evenings to make sure that in the morning it remains alight. I find it very fulfilling to come down in the morning and, gently blowing upon the coals, see them come alive again—to realise that, although the length of the night had seemed to snatch away the flame, the gentle blowing revives it.

So it is in life when the pressures of circumstances close in around us. The choices and decisions to be made may momentarily damp down the flame of fervour in our hearts, but they cannot steal it away. The gentle blowing of the wind of the Spirit will soon fan the flame of worship into life again.

It will be partly through corporate worship that this takes place—if it is truly Spirit-led. Somehow the oh-so-predictable song service, synthesised music and zealously animated worship leaders we so often encounter today leave me yearning for a different time, place and way. They are no more satisfying to me than the equally predictable liturgies of yesteryear.

How glad I am that I was privileged from my earliest Christian days to worship in a Christian community that knew how to respond fervently to the moving of the Holy Spirit from hearts burning with love for God.

How I loved those meetings! There was a divine unpredictability about them. Often the awesome sense of his presence found us reluctant to breathe or say anything; at other times strong men, most of them coal-miners, were prostrate on the floor in adoration of God. People would burst into songs of the Spirit and tears were allowed to flow without restraint.

We were all deeply conscious of the presence of God among us. We were caught up with the wonder, the breathtaking beauty, the immeasurable grace, the infinite greatness and the majestic splendour of God himself in our midst, our hearts aflame with him.

We were released by his presence into the reality of worship. It was as though our interaction in worship deepened, heightened and broadened our capacity to express worship together. It was from these times together that we went back to our homes and work filled by new visions of God.

When religion is stripped of its ritual and liturgy we return to the simplicity of our encounters and experience of God. Here in his burning presence our spirit is unimpaired in its approach to the throne. Here we see the glory of God before us. 'Blessed are the pure in heart, for they will see God' (Matthew 5:8).

It is such visions of God that made the ancient prophets what they were—mighty men of faith and the voice of God in their time. Here in the secret place of worship and praise where we behold him, we are being fitted for just such a calling to our own generation. Here is the vision that makes his ministers flames of fire.

'When Solomon finished praying, fire came down from heaven and consumed the burnt offering and the sacrifices, and the glory of the Lord filled the temple. The priests could not enter the temple of the Lord because the glory of the Lord filled it. When all the Israelites saw the fire coming down and the glory of the Lord above the temple, they knelt on the pavement with their faces to the ground, and they worshipped and gave thanks to the Lord, saying, "He is good; his love endures for ever" ' (2 Chronicles 7:1-3).

Thirty-two years ago God called me to be a preacher. My life has lived the joys of preaching ever since. I can't imagine anything that could excite the human heart to the same degree. There is a thrill in opening the Word of God and realising the awesome privilege of standing between God and men. There is also a fear of God causing the heart to tremble, the love of God causing the heart to reach out, and the anointing of God causing the mind to be alert to revelation and effective in communicating its truth.

I think all preachers would agree with me that we would be the first to fall back, not only in awe but in glad deference, should God sovereignly move in with a display of his presence, power and fiery burnings that made preaching at that moment unnecessary. He has done it before; he still does it at times.

While we were in the flow of worship one recent Sunday morning, God moved in upon us sovereignly in this fashion. There was such a work of the Spirit across the gathering that I knew it would be impossible to preach the Word that day. God had come.

Some were kneeling, some were standing, some were sitting. Some were prostrate before his presence. No-one dared try to call time on what was happening because God had taken the floor. And even without a preacher, that day twelve people came to Christ, acknowledging him as their Lord and Saviour.

As we left, our hearts burned with the flame of his presence.

12

Liberating love

You called, you cried, you shattered my deafness; you sparkled, you blazed, you drove away my blindness; you shed your fragrance and I drew in my breath, and I pant for you.

Augustine

I settled down in my seat, making myself comfortable for the train journey home from London to Yorkshire. As I did so, a young city gentleman took his seat opposite me. He was conservatively dressed in grey pinstriped suit, white shirt and club tie, and was carrying a briefcase and *The Times*. Throughout the journey he busied himself reading documents and making jottings in the margins of papers. Periodically he checked his watch, which suggested anticipation of what lay at the end of the journey.

Finally, the train slowed as it entered the station. He was already standing before it came to a halt, his briefcase closed, at the ready. I followed him on to the platform and out through the ticket barrier.

Suddenly, the city gentleman changed as a young woman rushed to meet him. Throwing her arms around him, she hugged and kissed him. Briefcase and *The Times* fell to the ground. In total disregard of the crowd of passengers pressing through, the two lovers gazed adoringly into each other's eyes. The rest of us moved on with knowing smiles.

There is something wonderfully abandoned about being in love. It frees the true self to emerge from behind the façade of conditioned personality. I looked back for a moment at the young couple, who were still holding each other in a loving embrace. All day they had been what was expected of them, but now they could show how they both felt—in love!

It's strange how we are so afraid of expressing emotion in relation to God for fear of being accused of emotionalism. It seems we are allowed to become emotional about everything and anything in life—except God.

Yet it is nothing new for people to misunderstand the extravagance of love. When Mary brought her jar of expensive perfume—a means of financial savings in those days—and poured it on Jesus' head and feet, Judas, whose heart had never felt this woman's love for Christ, regarded her action as a waste of money.

His cold, calculating mind saw her act of worship as religious fanaticism. He couldn't understand her passionate feelings of love for Christ. All he could see was the value of the perfume—a year's wages—much of which might have gone into his own pocket.

Mary's love expressed in this rush of affection and disregard of decorum troubled Judas's mean heart. To him, Jesus wasn't worth this 'waste' whereas, to Mary, Jesus was worth more than all she had in this world.

Our mind and affections will always concern themselves with what we value most. The person who fails to appreciate the Lord's worth can never engage in worship. If there is anything that occupies a higher priority in life than God, we tend to hold on to that, and whatever is lavished on him will appear a waste.

One of the most graphic images of David, the 'man after God's own heart', is that of the dancing king. He was leading the procession as Israel brought back to Jerusalem the ark of the covenant, which had for so long been in the hands of the Philistines.

68

For David, as for all Israel, the ark symbolised the presence of God among them. This was surely a time for rejoicing and great praise—God was again showing them his favour by returning to them this visible expression of his presence. David was unable to contain the ecstasy of the moment. Filled with the joy of the Lord, he leaped along the road in front of the procession.

Scripture records that David 'danced before the Lord with all his might, while he and the entire house of Israel brought up the ark of the Lord with shouts and the sound of trumpets . . . King David leaping and dancing before the Lord' (2 Samuel 6:14-16).

Whenever spiritual awakening has come to God's people, such vocal praise and extravagant exuberance has again made itself known.

I remember speaking, as a young teenager, with an elderly lady who had witnessed the Welsh revival. I recall the glow on her face as she described how the great chapels of the area had been filled with hundreds of people, some lying sobbing on the floor, others standing on seats and waving handkerchiefs, some shouting God's praise, some singing with their hands in the air.

To the cold-hearted such scenes are viewed as religious fanaticism and extremism, but in the presence of God it is none other than the liberation of the redeemed by grace. Such expressions of worship from freed hearts are spiritually acceptable because they are spiritually real.

I'm glad that worship in spirit and truth embraces the demonstration of our feelings. Feelings are the deepest and strongest motivations in our life. They are no cause for shame or fear. Even though our faith doesn't *rely* on feelings, it is nevertheless made the more joyous and warm because of them.

By faith Jesus performed miracles, but he let it be known that they were also the result of his being 'moved with compassion'. His teaching was similarly motivated: 'When Jesus landed and saw a large crowd, he had compassion on them, because they were like sheep without a shepherd. So he began teaching them many things' (Mark 6:34).

It is impossible for us to engage in any aspect of life without involving our emotions: anger or joy, peace or fear, happiness or disillusionment are the reasons for our attitudes and actions every day.

For too long we have been intimidated by conservatism, tradition and the fear of religious extremism. We need to express the pent-up feelings that have accumulated through days, weeks and in some cases years of either pain or happiness.

There is a time for silence, and for solitude, but these can never be experienced in their full richness unless they are counterbalanced by the release of the emotions and actions. We are not only creatures of mind and feeling, but of speech, gesture, touch, movement. Until the fulness of our created nature finds liberated expression in the abandonment of worship, our inner being remains unfulfilled and no act of worship is complete.

Many of the Hebrew words associated with worship show the wide variety of emotional responses involved in praise of God—shouting, raising of hands, bowing of the knee, prostration at his feet, joyous singing and dancing.

As well as being an expression of our liberty, worship is itself liberating. It allows the soul to express itself and, in the expression, to find the healing of God's love.

The psalmist expressed the feelings of liberated emotions in describing the Israelites' experience when God released them from captivity to return to their land: 'When the Lord brought back the captives to Zion, we were like men who dreamed. Our mouths were filled with laughter, our tongues with songs of joy. Then it was said among the nations, "The Lord has done great things for them" ' (Psalm 126:1-2).

To empty our worship of the expression of feeling is the same as robbing springtime of its flowers, nature of its colour, the birds of their song. Everything becomes dull and drab.

Our heartfelt worship is what clothes life with the colourful robes of majestic splendour, and gives to God the love he desires.

13

Healing love

Whether life is worth living depends on whether there is love in life.
R.D. Laing

The meeting had been long, but exciting. The people were so happy in praising God, which they had done with such enthusiasm, that those whose personalities were not free stood out in the crowd.

At the end of the meeting, among those who responded to the invitation to receive prayer, was a tall, fine-looking woman. She walked quickly to the front and stood trembling among the others, her fingers intertwined in a tight clasp. As I laid my hands on her to pray I could feel the tremor of tension through the body. Her face was strained and set.

I started to pray, asking God to lift the feeling of rejection, remove the spirit of heaviness and clothe her with a garment of praise. She trembled the more. I continued praying: 'Lord, may she know that you love her as she is, that you receive her because you love her, not for her performance in life.'

Suddenly her body began to shake and the stifled sounds of restrained weeping could be heard. I looked at her. The tears running down her pale face were bringing the mascara with them, forming dark rivulets. I continued to pray until I felt the trembling cease, calmness come. Now I looked and saw her lips quietly moving as she whispered, 'I love you, Lord. I love you, Lord. Thank you for your love.'

The hurting and the weeping had given way to healing and worship. Her soul was safe and secure in the knowledge of God's love, and now she was free to worship him.

At times we can feel ourselves trapped on the wheel of life, busied with busyness. Life becomes cold, demanding, frustrating, lonely. We find ourselves building a front before people, where the face smiles while the soul aches. Where the jovial laugh hides a crying heart.

Most of us have been concerned throughout life with what others think of us, and almost imperceptibly we have built up façades around the true self. We try to appear before others as we wish them to perceive us to be—which is rarely what we actually are. But in the presence of God it is impossible to maintain a pretence. Before the burning holiness of the Almighty, all that is untrue to ourselves disappears and what we are stands true before him.

John Steinbeck, the Nobel Prize-winning American novelist and playwright, in describing the way he came to terms with his true self, gave this account. 'I went into the mountains and stayed two years. I was snowed in eight months of the year and saw no-one except my two Airedales. There were millions of fir trees and the snow was deep and it was very quiet. And there was no-one to pose for anymore. You can't have a show with no audience. Gradually all the poses slipped off and when I came out of the hills I didn't have any poses anymore. It was rather sad, but it was far less trouble. I am happier than I have ever been in my life.'

We don't need to go to the mountains—just into the presence of God. In his presence there is no need for posing, no need for a façade. His love gently removes the spirit of heaviness, and his Spirit clothes us with the garment of praise. In the exhilaration of worship the healing hand touches the weary soul and renews it. What life has unravelled is woven afresh, what life has broken is put back together again. So effortlessly, while worshipping the Lord, the healing waters flow.

True worship can only come from the heart set free. Free to be oneself, to accept oneself, to know one is accepted and loved by God. Worship is the singing of the liberated lover running along hidden paths to rendezvous with the Beloved.

I have often been approached after preaching with the words, 'How did you know my situation? Who told you about me?' Others, after prayer, have said to me, 'You knew, didn't you?'

I've looked puzzled and replied, 'Knew what?', only to find they have been astonished at the accuracy of detail made known when praying for them. We need to realise: the God who made and redeemed us knows us through and through. He wants us to be aware of his intimate concern and love for us.

I recall walking at a convention among the people camped in the fields adjoining the auditorium—hundreds of tents and caravans with people making their lunches outside. Then I entered the cafeteria, where there must have been sixty or seventy people eating their lunch in groups, laughingly sharing the joys of the week.

It was there that I noticed her. She looked so miserable. Everyone else was bubbling with excitement and sharing their experiences, but she sat apart. She paid no attention to others. Indeed, it looked as though she was making a deliberate effort not to acknowledge that they were in the room. She ate her food with single concentration of mind.

'How strange,' I thought, 'amidst such happiness and joy to be so miserable.'

Within minutes of leaving the cafeteria I had forgotten all about her—until that evening, as we were worshipping in the meeting. During one of the songs of praise I noticed her, about three rows back. While everyone around was in an ecstasy of praise and worship, she stood transfixed, immobile, looking miserable, ensnared by the spirit of heaviness.

At the close of the preaching of the Word a large number of people came to be ministered to, among them this young

73

woman. I made my way deliberately towards her. I felt that not only was it imperative that she should touch God, but that I was best positioned at that moment to pray the prayer of release for her.

As I touched her forehead with my hand she just broke and the tears and sobbing became intense. I called for one of the lady counsellors near at hand to take her aside and share with her a little.

Later, I found out her story. As a young woman she had been dreadfully abused within her own family. She had been constantly put down and told she was ugly while her sister was pretty, that she was stupid while everyone else in the house was commendable. She was isolated within the family. As she grew up, she turned in upon herself more and more and began saying to herself the very things others had said to her. Inevitably, she ended up convinced she was unattractive, that no-one wanted her around, that no-one would ever love her. She wished she had never been born.

Then a friend at work, realising the sadness of her life, had reached out to her to share about Christ and invited her to come with them to this week-long convention. Before she realised what she was doing she had said yes, overwhelmed at being invited to come to *anything* with others.

The side of her that longed to be involved had grasped at the opportunity but she was soon thinking to herself, 'What have I done? What kind of week is it? Will there be many there? I'm sure I'll seem a misfit.' But feeling it was too late to withdraw, she had come.

She had been surprised to see the thousands of people around so happy and excited. But instead of rubbing off on to her, their enjoyment, because it was in such stark contrast to her own sad state, had made her feel more of a misfit than ever.

That night in the meeting I had closed the preaching with, 'Whoever you are, wherever you are, whatever you feel, God loves you, too.' That was the trigger of faith for her. She knew it was God speaking to her and she had come forward to turn her life over to him.

I can't begin to describe to you the difference it made. Over the next few days, whenever I saw that young woman she was laughing and smiling; happiness was all over her. It seemed as though the years of despairing misery were wiped away in a minute. She entered readily into the songs of praise and worship. In the fellowship of his presence and his people she had come alive with the beauty of the Lord.

God loves you, too. The love of God is the strongest motivation for our worship. We love him because he first loved us.

Erich Fromm wrote, 'Immature love says, "I love you because I need you." Mature love says, "I need you because I love you." ' It isn't the form of our worship, our posture in worship, the place of worship; it is the love of our heart extravagantly overflowing in gratitude to God that brings a smile to the face, happiness to the heart, and sprinkles the joy of God on others.

14

The secret of the Lord

The secret of the Lord is with those who fear him, and he will show them his covenant.

Psalm 25:14 RAV

Recently a friend of mine died. He was in many ways very different from me. Our backgrounds were dissimilar, but throughout the years we had been thrown together in so many situations that common bonds of love and affection had been forged that allowed us to be comfortable in each other's presence.

On hearing of his death I went into my study and sat in the darkened room. I didn't want others around me at this time. I wanted to be alone with my memories.

Looking back over those years, I recalled when he once sought me out in the field adjoining a convention site. As so often before, we sat together to talk. Suddenly, he said, 'Bryn, we've come a long way together, and although I know we're very different, I feel you're my friend. I want to share some things with you that I've never told others.'

With that, he opened to me the secret hopes and desires in his life. We shared as friend to friend.

How privileged I felt, yet how humbling to hear his secrets. But then this is how it is with the Lord: it is to those who have become his closest friends, to those worshipping souls that he opens up his secrets.

No example of this intimacy is clearer than that enjoyed between Enoch and God. God shared with him the secrets of his purposes, knowing that every disclosure was 'safe' with his friend. It was with Enoch that God shared his plan to have Jesus come a second time to earth—even before the first coming: 'Enoch ... prophesied ... "See, the Lord is coming with thousands upon thousands of his holy ones, to judge everyone" ' (Jude 14).

Their fellowship was so wonderful and fulfilling to God, he felt such compatibility with the heart of Enoch that one day, while they walked together, God decided to extend the journey on into heaven and Enoch never returned. 'Enoch walked with God; then he was no more, because God took him away' (Genesis 5:24).

Such deep friendships are not the result of occasional meetings; they develop gradually out of the sharing of life. Doing things together and going places together make us feel secure with each other. As the friendship deepens, trust develops to the point where we feel free to open up to each other the intimate details of our lives. It comes through having proven each other's integrity and drawn on each other's strength and loyalty in some of life's most difficult moments.

Significantly, it was only after three years with his disciples that Jesus called them his friends.

'You are my friends if you do what I command. I no longer call you servants, because a servant does not know his master's business. Instead, I have called you friends, for everything that I learned from my Father I have made known to you' (John 15:14-15). They were friends by virtue of the commitment they had shown, the experiences of life together they had enjoyed.

True friends don't require speech to enjoy their friendship. Presence is sufficient. They seem to anticipate each other's thoughts, instinctively knowing what pleases or disturbs each other. It is in those quiet, contemplative seasons of adoration of his Person, of worshipful delight in the majesty and love of God, that he chooses to disclose to us, his friends, the secrets of his counsel and covenant.

'The Lord confides in those who fear him; he makes his covenant known to them' (Psalm 25:14).

These quiet whispers of the Spirit are God's secrets. They are not meant to be shouted abroad, but held, believed, rejoiced in and talked over again in the secret place. There are things that I hold in the quietness of my heart that God spoke to me many years ago—promises, direction, glimpses of the future—that were not meant to be laid on others, but have continued to urge me forward, excite my heart and deepen my worship.

Mary, the mother of Jesus, knew what it was to have such whisperings of the Spirit and to hold them to herself: 'Mary treasured up all these things and pondered them in her heart' (Luke 2:19).

These shared intimacies don't take place in the crowd. God knows it requires stillness, where he can speak without our restless hearts interrupting. That is why he calls us into the secret place alone.

I once went alone to an idyllic spot down by a river, where it was so peaceful and quiet away from the crowds. I lay in the grass, my back warmed by the earth that had drunk from the sun shining down through the trees. Apart from the occasional bee buzzing in the clover, the air was still. It carried the sound of running waters tumbling over stones as they raced towards the waterfall below. I thought of his voice which, like the sound of many waters, had so frequently broken through the clamour of all around and hushed my restless soul.

Silence is not the world emptied of sound. It is to have your world filled with the stillness and hush of his presence. Speech would be an unwelcome intruder in the God-filled secret place. It is not that you have run out of things to say to him. It is simply that, at this moment, silence is your most eloquent form of speech.

Like a river, our worship can tumble or run still. It isn't that some people worship this way and others that way, according to their personality. That would mean worship was governed by our natural temperament. No, it is 'spirit and truth'. People's moods change—sometimes mellow, reflective, sober; at other times happy, extravagant, joyful. But every mood is an opportunity to express our worship. We worship him, not according to a stereotyped personality pattern, but in the spontaneity of the Spirit in every wholesome mood of life.

Sometimes, after listening to the car radio or a tape for some hours during a long journey, I switch it off and suddenly realise the silence again. It is often here in the worship-filled silence that God's secrets are shared with us.

This silence is not the emptiness of soul but the stillness of the inner being. Gone now are the rushing thoughts, the clashing senses, the active mind urging us to do something, the protesting priorities clamouring for attention. Here in his presence we have come to rest.

'Be still, and know that I am God; I will be exalted among the nations, I will be exalted in the earth' (Psalm 46:10). Stillness does not come easy in the contemporary world, where we are trained to assert ourselves to tackle our responsibilities. To efficient and diligent persons the thought of leaving the situation, of not *doing something*, is anathema. But with God, to be still is a great strength.

Moses discovered this in the great exodus of Israel from Egypt: 'Moses answered the people, "Do not be afraid. Stand firm and you will see the deliverance the Lord will bring you today. The Egyptians you see today you will never see again. The Lord will fight for you; you need only to *be still*" ' (Exodus 14:13-14).

It is in such times of seeming inactivity that we realise God is most active on our behalf. When we are the most quiet, his is the only sound to be heard—whispering the secret counsels of his heart and mind to us.

Possibly the question we most need to ask ourselves is not, 'Can we trust God with our secret longings and desires?' but, 'Can he trust us with his?'

15

Called to higher ground

I . . . had ambition not only to go further than any man had ever been before, but as far as it was possible for a man to go.

Captain James Cook

'Mrs Jones, Mrs Jones!' It was our neighbour calling over the garden wall to my mother. 'Is Bryn there, please? I need his help.'

As always, my mother readily volunteered me and I ran next door to see what was wanted.

'Come in quickly, Bryn,' said the neighbour, hurriedly shutting the door behind me. 'My budgie's got out of its cage.'

After feeding the bird she had forgotten to close the cage door, and now the bird was flying around the house. I felt awkward because I didn't like birds to be caged and never believed we should keep them that way. For the next ten minutes, although I tried to catch the bird, I was secretly hoping our mission would be in vain. I didn't want this beautiful bird to be caught.

As I went into the lounge she said, 'If it gets out it will die because it can't live in this climate.'

I couldn't help thinking, 'But wouldn't it be better to have a short life truly free than a long life imprisoned?' My dilemma was resolved, however, when the bird, flying up the stairs with the neighbour and myself in hot pursuit, escaped through an open bedroom window.

When truly free you can only be what your nature is, and a bird's nature is to fly, not to hop from perch to perch in a cage.

> The cage was not right.
> Its bars too restraining, its world too small.
> It was a prison.
> Out of its cage the bird rose naturally on the wing.
> It was born for flight, to climb the skies with songs of praise.
> It is a friend of the clouds, the wind and the air.

Worship has that same liberating effect upon the soul. When we are lost in the wonder of God's grace and goodness, worshipping the one whose beauty has captured our hearts, we discover we are not born again to be tied to this temporal world. In our liberated state we are most at home in his heaven.

Paul understood this experience. On at least one occasion he had been 'caught up into the third heaven'. Such was the fearful yet wonderful revelation of that time that an enraged enemy assaulted him in an effort to destroy the faith released by it. But the apostle found God's grace sufficient to enable him not to crumple under the pressure but to overcome in praise. He was a free man.

'[The Lord] said to me, "My grace is sufficient for you, for my power is made perfect in weakness." Therefore I will boast all the more gladly about my weaknesses, so that Christ's power may rest on me' (2 Corinthians 12:9).

On another occasion Paul and Silas were arrested and thrown into jail at Philippi. Mistreated and abused, they sat in the damp, airless dungeon, surrounded by cries of pain, fear and bitterness from other prisoners. Yet in that situation so little conducive to worship, the Bible says, 'About midnight Paul and Silas were praying and singing hymns to God, and the other prisoners were listening to them' (Act 16:25).

Little wonder what then happened. I plead guilty to the running away of my imagination at this moment, but in my

82

mind I can see the angelic hosts, stirred by these songs of praise, crowding into the cell. The heavenly choirs pressed in as the men continued in their worship until the whole place bulged at the seams, finally erupting when the doors burst open, the walls collapsed and the prisoners' chains dropped away!

To worship in Spirit is to find oneself strangely detached from the external pressures of life. Because you are joined to God, none of life's restrictions seem to have any bearing on what you are experiencing. Whatever your circumstances, you now find yourself baptised into a river of peace and tranquillity. The pressures of life clamouring to pull you down seem so far away. The worshipping lover of God is so God-conscious that, though his body may be imprisoned, his soul is like a bird set free.

Worship knows no prison, no chains, no locked doors—we are free to be, to love, to rise, to adore before his throne. Whenever we worship we are ascending higher into the presence of God. Things are very different in the hill of the Lord.

Mountains have always held a fascination for me. Not the extremely high ones that are unreachable to all except trained and skilful mountaineers, but the small mountains—or large hills, whichever you prefer to call them.

In summer months we have often taken the family for picnics 'up the mountains'. They have always been happy, boisterous times. One such occasion was one of those rare and beautiful days when the sun was shining but there was a pleasant, cooling breeze. We started up the long, sloping mountainside. At first, we made good headway, stopping every fifteen minutes or so to turn around and gaze at the view from the hillside, the children impatiently urging us to go higher.

Soon, their urgings ceased. It wasn't long before our youngest was too tired and wanted a piggyback. The others also wanted a turn. Their legs were aching, but still we pressed on. Now it was I who was urging them to continue—I felt we had come so far up, so why give up now?

'When you reach the top,' I said, 'it will be beautiful. When you get up there you'll see things you haven't seen before.' And so I kept urging them.

To their cries of 'How much further?' I would say, 'Oh, look, just a little further, we're almost there.' Then we would reach the point I had been indicating, only to find that the mountain sloped away and up another rise. Nevertheless we persevered and finally reached the top.

Everybody flopped down on the grass. We lay there for a few minutes, letting the sun shine warmly on us, everyone sighing and breathing deeply.

Finally, I looked up. 'My, it's terrific!' I exclaimed. 'What a beautiful view! How much more is visible up here than from down below.'

The children struggled to their feet to look and the eldest said, 'You're right, Dad. Everything looks different from up here.'

Sometimes we get too close to life to see it clearly. We become problem-conscious instead of God-conscious. We lose perspective in our situation. Molehills become mountains.

Psalms 120 to 134 are 'psalms of ascent', ever leading upwards to the presence of God in his temple. 'Who may ascend the hill of the Lord?' the psalmist asks elsewhere. 'Who may stand in his holy place?' (Psalm 24:3).

To worship in the mountain of God's presence enables us to see the way he has mysteriously and marvellously interwoven the circumstances of our lives. And here we will find that those very fingers that wrought the heavens and earth with such care now unravel the complexity of our twisted emotions.

Nothing need be to our loss. His love causes job, family, home and even hard times to find their place in his purpose, just as, from the mountain-top, fields, rivers and villages form a patchwork quilt across the earth.

16

Worship in the workplace

When man loses the sacred significance of work and of himself as worker, he soon loses the sacred meaning of time and life.
Carl F.H. Henry

John was a hard-working farmer. Whenever you met him, his face was wreathed in smiles, his eyes blue and twinkling, his complexion clean and ruddy.

I used to love going to help him at weekends. He had one of those farms which was too small to employ additional labourers yet too large to manage alone, and so my weekend help was greatly appreciated. He had thirty-two milking cows. He had no milking-machines so he would start at one end of the parlour and I at the other, milking each cow by hand.

That milking-parlour often became a house of worship, John's rich tenor voice leading us both as we sang, praised and laughed together, even as we emptied the milk-pails into the cooler. Then, singing the praises of God, we would return to more milking.

I was learning with John that worship embraces the ordinary day-to-day experience of our lives. Worship must not be severed from the rest of our human activities; it ought to pervade and dominate every routine in our daily duty, for God is 'in all and through all and over all'.

This time-space world is an infant-school classroom of our emerging human spirit. It is here in the school of life that our spiritual capacity is developed to appreciate the wonder of God's person and to prepare us for our privilege of co-sovereignty with him in the coming age.

Our awareness of God's love and kindness, of God's strength and mercy, of God's goodness and favour, are all provoked by the daily experiences of our lives. The heart has nothing of God to sing about unless it has been proven in the workshop of life.

The prophet Zechariah saw what in foretaste we already experience: the closing of the gap between secular and spiritual life that will mark the great end-time revival destined to cover the earth. All of life becomes spiritual—the kitchen and workshop are as much sanctuaries for the presence of the Most High God as any cathedral or church building: 'On that day HOLY TO THE LORD will be inscribed on the bells of the horses, and the cooking pots in the Lord's house will be like the sacred bowls in front of the altar' (Zechariah 14:20).

Sometimes people think that preachers or pastors have a special place in the heart of God beyond others, that somehow these 'holy people' find it easier to enjoy fellowship with God because they are close to him throughout the day. Such people see themselves, by contrast, as disqualified from intimate fellowship with God because they have to 'go to work in the world'.

It is a strange idea, because none of us can isolate ourselves from the world around. Indeed, it would not be desirable. Jesus himself said, 'My prayer is not that you take them out of the world but that you protect them from the evil one' (John 17:15).

God wants every individual equally to enjoy unbroken fellowship daily with him. Our worship is not to be confined to special days and special places. Worship has to do with the spirit of a person enjoying and loving God in the normal flow of life.

I am sure Joseph's carpenter's shop in Nazareth was filled with the praise and worship offered by Jesus and the other apprentices who worked alongside him learning their trade. People must have been blessed simply by walking into such an atmosphere of joy and thanksgiving, free of rancour, grumbling and gossip. Jesus knew what it was to live in worship in the everyday flow of life in this world.

Aquila and Priscilla experienced the same thing while making their tents, surrounded by the cosmopolitan atmosphere of the city of Corinth. The hustle and bustle of commerce, the labour and sweat of the poor, the poverty and pain in the inner city ghettoes, the drunkenness and loose morals. Yet they continued their task with worship-filled hearts, for the sanctuary of God was within them.

God reveals himself not only in times of solitary meditation but also in the circumstances of daily life. Each situation affords opportunity for a new unfolding of his power and wisdom, some new experience of his grace and kindness, some new demonstration of his greatness and ability, some fresh appreciation of his worth—until we are 'lost in wonder, love and praise'.

Alan was one of the finest men of God I've ever known, devoting his life to serving God and God's people. But he was not a pastor; he was a joiner in an electrical firm. Everyone knew where he stood. His testimony was one of an uncompromising Christian lifestyle.

Boldly he would testify in street meetings, preaching faithfully and fearlessly the salvation of Christ for all people. But the thing I remember most about him was the long hours we would spend together in worship and prayer before God. I would grow tired but he seemed born for these sacred hours. He was as filled with vigour and life after half a night as when we'd first begun.

Again and again he would say to me, 'Bryn, boyo, I love God more than life. I'd rather worship him that do anything else on earth.'

Wherever you are, in office, factory, home, school, college, university—God is there, for God is in you. Nothing outside of you is greater than the God who is in you. Everything you touch can have the stamp of holiness placed upon it. Your life and faith create the environment necessary for you to worship in spirit and in truth.

The way you do your work, your attitudes towards your colleagues, can all express your love and heart for God.

Paul described worship as part of the thanksgiving process of our lives (Romans 12:1-2)—thanksgiving for every ordinary experience, not only for the 'spiritual' things. Worship makes it *all* spiritual.

Worship leads us away from a preoccupation with ourselves and our self-conditions and directs our attention towards Christ. Worship is not egocentric but Christocentric. But this doesn't mean that we need to leave our legitimate responsibilities in life in order to find him. Wherever we are, there Christ is, and whatever we are engaged in, Christ desires to be fully involved in it. He is not only the Christ of the heavens but the Christ of the workplace.

When he left his Father's presence to come to earth he laid aside the majestic splendour that was rightfully his in the heavens. In becoming a man he assumed the responsibilities true to men and women. By being a carpenter he was not any the less God, but signified to men and women that God is entirely comfortable in the carpenter. This would be equally true had he been an accountant, an electrician, a computer analyst or a business executive.

We must not think that the workplace is alien to God, but recognise that he is as much at home in the workplace of our legitimate responsibilities as he is in the highest heavens.

Work was something God was engaged in before man was created. Indeed, men and women are the result of God's work. Work is not a consequence of the fall of man; it was part of God's and man's experience before the fall.

In becoming a carpenter, Christ sanctified the workplace, illustrating to us by his own labours that work is the place for the holy as much as for the skilled. We need to be filled with the Spirit to do our daily work as much as we need to be filled

with the Spirit to preach the gospel of Christ.
 And in our work, we worship him.

17

Heaven and earth are one

To have faith is to have wings.
James M. Barrie

'Throw me the ball!' one child called.

'No, to me, to me!' shouted another.

All the children were excited. It was a beautiful summer day for our picnic by the river. Families were chatting away happily, busily unpacking their picnic lunches while the children played. It was warm and peaceful.

Suddenly I saw a commotion develop just along the river-bank. One little girl had waded through a very shallow part of the river to the other side. Then she had moved along the bank as she played, only to find, now that she wanted to come back, that the water was deeper here. The frightened child was crying, shouting for Dad's help. Mother was trying to calm her down, but there were so many other voices saying different things that the child was becoming increasingly confused and upset.

Then the child's father waded out with several other young men, forming a line across the river, and laughingly picked up the child and passed her along the line. By the time she was put down on the bank she too was laughing; the fear all gone. A living bridge had made both sides one.

Who has not at times felt the cold hand of fear in adverse circumstances? Then our fear has increased because, when we have gone before the Lord, he has seemed so distant—like the child's father on the far bank, with what seems like an unbridgeable gulf between. In our confusion we cannot think of any reason for this feeling. Deep down we know God is not fickle or temperamental, so we feel bewildered.

It is here we discover that in exercising our *priestly* ministry we close the door on fear. God has made us a holy priesthood: 'You . . . like living stones, are being built into a spiritual house to be a holy priesthood, offering spiritual sacrifices acceptable to God through Jesus Christ' (1 Peter 2:5).

Don't be frightened by the word 'priest'. In Latin it is *pontifex,* meaning 'bridge-builder'. In everyday experience our priestly ministry of worship bridges the gap between heaven and earth. Time and space are no longer governing factors. The Spirit has bridged the two worlds.

The spiritual sacrifices we offer him are our surrendered life and God-centred praise and adoration. We worship him from a love-filled heart. And as we worship, our heart is stilled, the fears dispelled and the love of God fills our soul.

'Fear not' are two of the most frequently used words of Jesus. Fear gives us a distorted view of our circumstances, suggesting all kinds of gruesome possibilities. At times there appears to be an unholy conspiracy between our circumstances, feelings and mind. They work together to paint pictures of possible outcomes to our situation that can be quite terrifying.

As a child I would often visit my grandmother for several weeks during the summer holidays. She lived in a little cottage along an old disused railway line, right out in the country. When coming home from the town, the bus would drop me by the little river about half a mile from the house, and I would have to walk the rest of the way. The narrow, winding path between the trees was great fun in broad daylight, but if I was late back and dusk fell, the whole scene changed. The moon cast shadows that turned the trees into giants. The wind in the branches became moaning creatures of the night. In the rustling of the leaves I envisaged a monster creeping after me.

I would run as fast as my legs could carry me, arriving at the house out of breath, to be greeted by Gran, who covered her anxiety with a stern look because she had warned me to get home well before dusk. Now she would be waiting for my excuses.

'You were afraid. You've been running again.'

I would try to steady my heavy breathing and pretend that I hadn't been afraid, that like a big man I had walked all the way.

Of course, the following day in the bright sunshine I would play among those same trees, shooting at the crab-apples with my catapult. In the daylight there were no monsters that I couldn't deal with.

The unknown, the darkness, the night sounds all conjure up ills that will never be. But the worshipping soul knows what it is to dwell constantly in the light of God, where fear has no place, where grace reassures, where life is secure, where hope dwells serene.

The night-time circumstance can become a God-filled hour. You can find with the psalmist that God can visit you amid your pressures and bring peace where fear would try to control. Instead of the trembling of fear there can be the song of praise: 'By day the Lord directs his love, at night his song is with me—a prayer to the God of my life' (Psalm 42:8).

Worship draws us into the consciousness of his presence where fear cannot stay. God is *always* with us. There is never a moment when we need fear that he has left us alone.

During the day it is easy to forget the moon and stars. We think only of the clouds and the sun, or the blue sky, because we tend to be aware only of the visible. That's why, at night, no-one remembers the sun. We think instead of the blackness of the night and the brightness of the stars.

But paradoxically, we are often most conscious of the invisible

God during times of pressure and difficulty. Seeing the dark circumstances, we cry out for the sunshine of his presence. It is at our point of need that we become most aware of our inability to handle our situation and therefore look to him who is invisible.

It is in the night-time of life that the glory of his person shines the brightest. This does not mean he isn't there in the good times. He is there at all times and we need to train ourselves to walk not by sight but by faith.

It is worship that makes us conscious of the reality of his person and presence at all times. I remember this lesson coming home to me during a long and exhausting ministry trip. Sometimes people have a wrong idea of itinerant ministry. They see it as travelling to exotic lands, with plenty of opportunity to see the world. The reality is often very different. I have frequently visited countries where, from the moment of arrival, I have seen only the inside of meeting-rooms, and by the time I board the plane home, all I have seen of the country has been on the drive from airport to house or hotel and back.

This particular ministry trip was like that. From the moment I stepped off the plane I had been rushed from one meeting to the next. I had been away two weeks and was feeling intensely the absence of my wife and children. I longed to be with them again. I had spoken on the telephone but that had only served to make me miss them more acutely.

This evening I had retired to my room early and was listening to the sounds of the family downstairs enjoying themselves, children and parents laughing together. I felt the intense loneliness of those who spend a great deal of time on the road, be it salesmen, business executives, preachers, politicians, whatever. As the happy conversations continued downstairs, I imagined what each member of my own family back home might be doing at that moment.

Quietly I turned to the Lord and allowed him to fill my mind with a sense of his presence. 'Father,' I said, 'I'm so alone at this moment.'

Before I could say any more, I seemed to sense his smile, and quietly the inner voice said, 'Not alone, surely? I'm here with you. Enjoy fellowship with me.'

I remembered how, years before, I had been four weeks non-stop holding an evangelistic campaign in which many people had found Christ. Every day there had been folk to be counselled and followed up. Though so busy, I had felt so alone. Then I had received a letter from an old man who prayed regularly for us, and he closed his letter with these words: 'May the smile of God be ever upon you.'

That's our God. We're never alone—his smile is ever upon us. And with that remembrance, my heart swelled with love for God and in that lonely bedroom I worshipped.

18

Strength and beauty

This is the test of your manhood: How much is there left in you after you have lost everything outside of yourself?
Orison Swett Marden

He stood before us tall, erect and strong-featured, the clear skin stretched tightly over his face bearing the telltale 'blue' marks of coal burns. His eyes were dark and intense, his powerful shoulders supporting his upraised arms in praise to God.

Evan was a coalminer who was every inch a man's man. No-one could call him weak. This was why other strong men respected him; he could cut and move as much coal as the strongest of them. But at the same time his character was gentle and warm—he loved God and his fellow-man. Young men, myself included, aspired to know, love and worship God as he did. His mixture of strength and warmth attracted us.

The psalmist introduces us to a similar strange yet wonderful combination in describing his sense of the divine presence while in worship: 'Splendour and majesty are before me, *strength and beauty* are in his sanctuary' (Psalm 96:6 NASB).

Splendour and majesty we can understand—with their tone of regal splendour they seem fitted for each other. But strength and beauty seem such strange twins. Strength is firm, set, determined, unmoved and unbending, whereas beauty suggests itself to be gentle, yielding, soft, exquisite, tender.

The psalmist discovered in worship that these two seeming opposites are perfectly woven together in the nature of God. In the gospels we again see them equally balanced in the life of Christ. The strength of resolve and conviction undergirded his zeal in driving out the money changers from the temple: 'In the temple courts he found men selling cattle, sheep and doves, and others sitting at tables exchanging money. So he made a whip out of cords, and drove all from the temple area, both sheep and cattle; he scattered the coins of the money changers and overturned their tables' (John 2:14-15). Yet how tenderly he shared eternal life with the outcast woman at the well in Samaria!

Again, we see his strength in his unyielding and determined embrace of the final week of his earthly ministry, culminating in the cross at Calvary. And in the very midst of his sufferings the tenderness of his heart is expressed in his words from the cross, 'Father, forgive them, for they do not know what they are doing.'

Down the years, artists have attempted to capture on canvas the image of strength and beauty which the gospels have painted of Christ, but none has been able to achieve it.

But *we* can see it. How blessed we are to gaze on him, to love him, to bathe in the glory of his presence within ourselves. Here in worship we discover the strength to resist any thoughts of quitting. We are spiritually refreshed and equipped with a new determination to overthrow the powers of darkness and drive out demons as we advance the kingdom of God.

The psalmist, enthralled by the beauty of God's person, longed to be for ever lost in the wonder of it all: 'One thing I ask of the Lord, this is what I seek: that I may dwell in the house of the Lord all the days of my life, to gaze upon the beauty of the Lord and to seek him in his temple' (Psalm 27:4).

While strength and beauty may be physical characteristics, I am using the terms here in a different way. I am referring to the inner resolve in times of adversity and the inner beauty of a person's character.

Some years ago, while engaged in a neighbourhood visitation programme, I knocked on the door of a small terrace house, to have the door opened by the sweetest old lady you could ever wish to meet. Her hair was snow-white, her skin clear. There were wrinkles around her smiling eyes.

My friend and I explained that we were holding evangelistic meetings nearby and were visiting the area to share the love of Christ with people.

She smiled warmly saying, 'Wonderful. Would you like a cup of tea?'

We were most pleased, because that had certainly not been the usual greeting that day. We went inside and sat in her neat sitting-room. The kettle was already simmering on the kitchen stove, and within a few minutes we were talking happily, eating a biscuit and drinking our tea.

'I'm a Christian already, you know,' she said. 'That's why I'm so thrilled you've come to the village to share the Lord. I've prayed for a long time that someone would come and hold meetings in this village.'

Looking at her I said, 'Well, tell us your story', for it was clear to me that the richness of her life had a story of grace to tell.

For a few moments she sat quietly with the faraway look of one searching her memory. Then she told us how she and her husband had both found Christ and started bringing up their children in the Christian way. Then the coming of the last war had changed her life dramatically: in one week she had received three telegrams from the War Office informing her that first her husband, and then each of her two sons, had been killed in action. In one terrible week her whole family had been snatched from her.

I sat stunned, quieted by her story, and found myself saying,

99

'In one week you lost everyone?'

'Oh no, not everyone,' she replied. 'Jesus was still with me and still is. I've never felt alone. I don't understand why it all happened, but then I leave that with God. I thank him for his presence and love that is always with me.'

When we left her little home that afternoon I felt humbled by the strength and beauty we had seen and touched in this woman.

For millions of people it is a cold, hard and often painful journey through life. But for those who have become lovers of God in worship there is in God's love a healing balm for every grief, a strengthening hand for all who are weak and a grace sufficient to enable us to go forward victoriously in life, turning every intended stumbling-block into a stepping-stone to new and higher ground.

On another occasion, one Sunday morning, I remember the feeling of momentary shame that came on me. I was standing alongside Graham in the worship service. He was a businessman with a deep, open love for God, though his life had been marked by tragedy. His brother had committed suicide at a time of deep depression, while his aged mother had been bedridden for years. Single-handed, Graham had struggled on, maintaining the family business and caring for his mother without ever complaining at his lot in life.

That week I had been grumbling at having to work overtime to cover for a sick colleague when there were other things I had so much wanted to do. And now the person I found myself standing alongside in the morning service was Graham. His inner strength and beautiful worship melted me. I realised there and then that worship must fill the life before it can cross the lips.

Quietly I bowed my head and whispered, 'Lord, forgive me.'

People often ask what place of worship we attend, or what is our form of worship. Yet these are not the real issues. Much more important is our attitude of heart and mind as we worship.

The Word teaches that we are created in the image and likeness of God. That's why the more like him we become, the more of his own strength and beauty we reflect and the more in keeping with our eternal heritage and destiny we feel.

19

Exploring new worlds

You see things; and you say, 'Why?' But I dream things that never were; and I say, 'Why not?'
George Bernard Shaw

The school was less than a mile away but frequently my mother would have to come looking for me, knowing very well that once again the park pond had lured me! I should have been home in fifteen minutes, but it often took me well over an hour.

To me the park pond was a world of its own. I would press my face close to the water to create the shadow that allowed me to look down into the underwater world. The world of sticklebacks, redthroats, waterboatmen, tadpoles and newts. It was all there in our park pond. I would gaze entranced while time slipped by, wondering what that underwater world was like to live in.

Why were they all so different, I wondered, and how could so many different creatures get on so well? Did they fight? How many meals did they eat each day? I never saw waterboatmen drink. How could they dive under water and stay there for so long without breathing? A child's questions, which may seem silly to the knowledgeable adult, but for me then it was all so mysterious and wonderful.

I even kept my own mini-pond, resplendent with creatures taken home in a tin from the much larger park pond. Everything went well—until the day one of my newts escaped, making its way up our neighbour's drain. She came round asking for help to remove a 'strange-looking creature' in her bath! I didn't dare admit it was my newt, and even got sixpence for picking the creature up and removing it.

We were all happy: she with the newt's removal, me with the sixpence-worth of sherbert and liquorice, and the newt with being back in its pond.

The child's world is one of constant adventure. Who has not smiled at the little girl wheeling her pram, talking to her doll as though it were alive? Or laughed at the boy tumbling down the street as he fights with an imaginary invasion of evil aliens from another planet, then suddenly stopping and throwing his arms in the air like some great conqueror surveying the slain on the field of battle?

I wonder what Jesus had in mind when he said, 'Truly I say to you, unless you are converted and become like children, you shall not enter the kingdom of heaven' (Matthew 18:3 NASB)? Was he just teaching the simplicity of faith, or was he hinting at the seeing of the kingdom within oneself that requires the child's imaginative eye?

The order and choice of words is significant. He didn't say, 'Unless you become like a child and become converted.' It is the other way round: the childlike attitude is developed *after* conversion. Is he inferring that there is a rediscovery of imagination and adventure associated with the faith that enters the kingdom, a childlike faith that sees the invisible, and acts as though the invisible were visible?

As far back as I can remember, I have been a dreamer. I don't mean the usual 'cheese dreams' or late-night video-shows of the subconscious, but the wide-awake dreaming of the mind—visualising what things *could* be as opposed to what things are. I mean the seeing of potential far greater than what is currently

104

visible.

My wife and I, in every move of home, have bought an old property, not because we love living in dilapidated buildings, but because we have seen character in a property fallen into disrepair. We have seen what it could be, once restored.

All the great accomplishers of history have been men and women who have learnt to dream, to visualise, to see beyond the present and reach into the future with a faith that has caused the dream to become a reality.

The dreamer is well-known throughout the Scriptures. As God revealed himself to the hearts of men, their minds were opened to see, and their lives thereafter became a pursuit of what they had seen.

Moses came down from Sinai to make a tabernacle in the wilderness according to the pattern he had seen on the mountain. Joseph, in all the hardships of the jails of Egypt, remembered a dream that one day his brothers would bow down before him. It was that dream that prevented his becoming vindictive or bitter, so that when, years later, they did stand before him, he was able to say, 'It was not you who sent me here, but God.' That's the dreamer.

The prophets' dreams became their prophesying, as they spoke of a return from captivity for God's people, of the glory of the latter house being greater than that of the former. Jesus gave the commission to continue the blessing of God to the ends of the earth to a small core of people who believed in him. He saw in them the harvest of the world. Paul saw the purpose for which Christ had laid hold of him and was now in pursuit of that dream with all his might.

All lovers of God are dreamers. Those who worship most love most, and those who love most dream often.

This is what we see with the woman who had been sick with an issue of blood for twelve years. Having spent all her money on private physicians, she was no better for it. Then she heard about Jesus. 'She came up behind him in the crowd and touched his cloak, because she thought, "If I just touch his clothes, I will be healed" ' (Mark 5:27-28).

Was she not already seeing herself whole, healthy, strong, able to cope with life again? Before she even ventured out of the house into the crowd, her faith had ventured imaginatively into wholeness.

With what excitement Abraham began his journey to the promised land! Even while he packed his tent to begin the nomadic, pilgrim life, his eye of faith was already looking down through the generations to light upon a city whose builder and maker was God. It was the seeing of that city that enabled him to endure the tent.

We can enjoy the unseen world of God's purposes in our present age. The yet-to-unfold ages of the future, filled with the exciting prospect of co-operation with God, yield their mystery to those whose faith explores beyond the visible. Those who dare to venture beyond that veil find their spirit leaping to lay hold of what their faith sees—and their heart overflows with worship.

Why does sadness mark so many people's lives in adult years? Often it is simply because, somewhere in the harsh experiences of life, they have lost the adventure of a child's exploring mind. Imagination and wonder have died at the hand of the harsh rebuffs of life. They have now become slaves of the sophisticated, intellectual adult world, their lives filled with cares and worries.

The soul ceases to praise when it loses its sense of adventure. Worship ends when mystery and wonder die in the heart of man. But where they are retained, the quickened mind, the released affections are all drawn upwards towards the mysterious beauty with which God has clothed himself.

I remember, one winter, peering through the windows. It was beautiful outside. The snow was still falling, laying down a thick white carpet on the roads, and clothing the hedgerows and trees with a matching coat.

'Come on,' I said, 'let's go out and be the first to leave our tracks.'

My wife and I, and the four children, excitedly put on our warm clothing and boots, and set out.

Everything was so soft, still and silent. The familiar landmarks in the hedgerows were covered over. We were in our well-known neighbourhood, but everything looked different, fresh and new, and we were pioneers again, the first to blaze a trail.

After a while the falling snow eased and we returned home again by the trail we'd left behind us. Once indoors we huddled around the open fire, laughing and sharing stories while drinking our hot tea.

How refreshing it is to explore new paths of worship—to blaze fresh trails of exuberant thanksgiving. Let's be adventurous pioneers of praise. Let's cultivate our liberty in worship by stirring ourselves in the adventure of spontaneity.

We must safeguard the spontaneity of our approach to God. Ritualistic elements, however attractive initially, will inevitably weave a thread of death into the mantle of worship.

20

What is man?

Slightly lower than the angels is a whole lot better than slightly higher
than the apes. Let's get the order straight.
Stuart Briscoe

'What is man that you are mindful of him?' (Psalm 8:4).

Throughout the day we had driven along the winding roads
that ridge Colorado's great canyons. Breathtaking views had
lured us from the vehicles again and again to take photographs,
seeking to capture the awesome beauty of the moment. Now,
night-time had fallen. The clear blue sky had turned inky black,
and millions of stars were shining down on us.

My thoughts moved out across the expanse of space,
marvelling at the greatness, the vastness of God's creation. I
found myself asking question after question: Are there other
worlds beyond our own? Are they inhabited? How many other
galaxies are out there? What purpose had God in mind in such
a vast creation? Could he produce so much and yet confine
his concerns to this little planet, Earth?

Will the future age, I wondered, unfold the prospect of our
serving God's purpose beyond this earth? Where are the outer
boundaries of these created heavens?—they cannot be infinite,

for they were created. And, outside their boundary, will we meet him who has no boundary, the infinite God?

But the one persistent thought that pushed its way through every question was: How could God, so vast, so great, concern himself with the details of our personal welfare? 'What is man that you are mindful of him?'

That illustrious preacher, Joseph Parker, once said of the greatness of God in relation to our world: 'He sees the universe like a trembling dewdrop on a leaf of a flower.'

But, amazingly, this does not mean he is too great to be concerned for us. On the contrary, Jesus assured his anxious disciples that they had no reason to be concerned for food, drink, clothing or shelter. He drew their attention to the birds and the lilies of the field, emphasising God's concern and care for them, and he reminded the disciples how much more they were worth to the Father in heaven.

We cannot help but worship a God who loves us with such intensity, cares for us with such faithfulness, and concerns himself with such detail of our lives.

David, as a shepherd boy on the hills of Bethlehem, would sing out God's praise by night as well as by day. Sometimes he would be startled by the sounds of unseen predators approaching his flock or the screech of the night owls. What often helped quiet his heart was to gaze up at the stars, seeing them as the bright-robed choirs and orchestral musicians of the night. As he sang his spiritual songs they seemed to shine more brightly, swaying together in dance.

'What is man,' he would think, 'that you are mindful of him?' Then, sighing deeply, 'Thank you, God!'

While living in Guyana, I recall once feeling utterly drained of energy. The oppressive heat and humidity seemed to take one's breath away.

But that wasn't all. There seemed to be a million mosquitoes to every cubic inch of space! Culturally, I felt a total misfit. I was surrounded by the continuous haunting sounds of Hindu music. I was confronted on every hand with poverty and sickness on a massive scale. The food was completely different.

Everything conspired to make me feel a total stranger, and I longed for the friends I had left in England—to be back where things were comparatively comfortable. I felt so homesick and lonely that night.

Finally, I got into the Volkswagen and drove down to the beach. I walked along the seafront and, sitting beneath a palm tree, looked up at the vast expanse of starlit sky.

I recognised the Plough, the Bear, the Lion. I looked out over the ocean bathed in soft moonlight and recalled how, as a student, I had done the same from the sand dunes of Swansea. Suddenly, I realised this was the same sky, same stars, same moon and, above all, the same God who was over me, and I didn't feel lonely any more. I sat there quietly praising and worshipping before returning home refreshed.

I have never faced those feelings since. I discovered there that, wherever you are and whatever your circumstances, God is always present to be worshipped.

We must never slip back to the state of mind we were in before we met Christ, when God, if he existed at all, was a vague figure who lived a billion miles away. One of the great mysteries of our experience of him is that the God who created all outside of us, and who rules it from the highest heaven, has made his home within us. At no time will that change. Our experience of it may change, but never the reality of it.

One day on holiday I was sunbathing on the beach with my eyes closed, enjoying the warmth from the sun-drenched blue sky above me. Suddenly it darkened, and I shivered. My first ridiculous thought was, 'Oh, the sun's gone away!' But peering through my eyelids, I realised, of course, that a cloud had simply come between me and the sun. The breeze blew it along and within half a minute I was again enjoying the full warmth of the sun.

How often we say, 'Oh, God has left me!' But the reality is that, just like the sun, God hasn't moved. It is merely that something has clouded our fellowship. And often it is in worship and praise that one has felt the winds of God blow away the things between. God knows our hearts. He readily

111

responds to our love and desire for unmarred fellowship with him.

Sometimes the cloud is one of feeling unworthy in his presence. I remember one such occasion when I felt so cast down about myself. All day I had been aware of my weaknesses and frailty, turning over in my mind how unlike God I was in disposition and character. I longed to please him and to bear his image but somehow I felt so unworthy, unclean.

I think the nearer you approach to God, the more accurately you see yourself, and the more unlike him you feel yourself to be.

The fact was, I had been wrong in the way I had spoken back to a young man who had shared his convictions about the work we were involved in. He had expressed what he believed was wrong with it, what other people were saying, where we were making mistakes and, as I had listened to it all, I had felt indignation rising up inside me.

'What right does he have to speak to me like this?' I thought. 'He's never helped us in this work, he's never become involved. Who's he referring to when he says all these other people are saying these things? And what if they are? I prefer my way of doing God's work than their way of *not* doing it.'

My thoughts turned to words, in the rough response, 'There are always those who criticise what others do, while doing nothing themselves.' And so I rationalised the charges against us.

But the young man persisted, until finally I reacted with, 'Get out! I don't want you with your negatives!'

As soon as he'd gone I realised that my reaction had been unrighteous. I felt miserable. 'I can't come before God with an attitude like this,' I said to myself, so I slunk around doing my work, feeling a long way from him.

It's a common misunderstanding—delaying our entry into God's presence because we think that any attempt to come before him in such a state would not be welcome. How wrong I was. Later that evening, as I sat quietly in the room, I turned my heart to the Lord and said, 'God, I'm sorry for reacting the way I did, sorry for the person I've been.'

Instantly, I felt the warmth of his presence. I didn't feel pushed away or held at bay.

'Lord,' I said, 'please forgive me for my wrong reactions.'

Immediately, I knew I was forgiven. I felt his peace. I would seek out the young man and ask his forgiveness. But then my mind reacted: 'It shouldn't be as easy as this. I ought to be more miserable. I ought to somehow pay for this wrong I've done. I don't want to find myself indulging in the self-deception of cheap grace.'

Quietly the inner voice said, 'But I'm not like that.'

It dawned on me then how many of us are trapped in wrong images of God and how much we miss of life, its happiness and its joys because of it. We live too long in misery, feeling that, since we have failed him, God will not be in any hurry to welcome us back into his presence. We are afraid to rejoice instantly in forgiveness lest it seem too easy, too cheap.

But God isn't like that. He longs for us to come. Indeed, in worshipping in his presence we find cleansing for our soul, as did Isaiah, who stood before the Lord in the temple and was touched on his unclean lips by the coals from the altar.

We must not worship a God of our own making, a God made in the image of man. We must learn to worship in spirit and in truth, which is to love, rejoice and worship him for who he is, not what we think he might be. When God forgives he doesn't keep us in a spiritual isolation block to deprive us of the sense of blessing. He's not like that. He is swift to receive us, instant to forgive us, ready to love us, longing to bless us.

Whenever you feel threatened, perplexed by what is happening to you, remember that the same fingers that wove the heavens together are weaving the threads of love and life, grace and glory in the wonderful mystery of the divine purpose for *you*.

When earth threatens, consider the heavens and cry out joyfully, 'What is man? What am I? But thank you, God!'

21

Worship
and sacrifice

The summit of worship is a life laid down.
Anon.

Thousands had fled the burning township, clutching their
children as they raced for their lives. For months racial tensions
had been high between the black and Indian communities. Then
the rumour spread that a black family had been attacked. The
reaction was swift and terrible. Within the hour hundreds of
homes were ablaze.

The Indian community fled the district, thousands making
their way downriver to escape the violence and hatred. The
government sent in troops to restore calm, but there hung in
the air a mixture of shame and fear. Behind the sea wall, the
homeless Indians started building shacks with pieces of timber,
cardboard, tin and any other materials they had been able to
salvage from the ruins.

Within weeks the thousands of squatters had erected a new
township of squalor. When the church gathered for prayer,
moved by the plight of the refugees, I suggested that we all
should give what we could to help these poor people.

As we worshipped and prayed, an elderly widow came forward. I knew her well. She lived alone, having never had children. Her house had none of the comforts and conveniences that most of us take for granted. To bring brightness and colour to the bare boards of her house, she had pasted pictures from old magazines on the wall.

That night she dropped a small paper bag on to the table where we were placing our offerings. Later, when I gathered them up, I found that her paper bag was two-thirds full of rice. I knew that, small as it was, this offering probably represented all she had. Yet it was not given reluctantly or with murmuring. She had made her sacrifice with the peace and joy of a worshipping heart.

The first mention in the Scriptures of the word 'worship' is in Abraham's offering of Isaac upon the altar. In restraining his servants from accompanying them to Mount Moriah, he said, 'Stay here with the donkey while I and the boy go over there. We will worship and then we will come back to you' (Genesis 22:5).

Abraham never considered that he and Isaac would not return. He was not about to indulge in some misguided act of religious zealotry. Nor did he view the sacrifice of Isaac upon an altar as in some way appeasing a savage God. Abraham was confident that his sacrificing of Isaac would not be to loss but to gain, that the boy would live.

'By faith Abraham, when God tested him, offered Isaac as a sacrifice. He who had received the promises was about to sacrifice his one and only son . . . . Abraham reasoned that God could raise the dead, and figuratively speaking, he did receive Isaac back from death' (Hebrews 11:17-19).

The first mention of any topic in Scripture often gives a clue to its broader spiritual significance. By this principle, worship and sacrifice are for ever linked.

Whenever we worship it is with a desire to give over to God something we feel we cannot keep to ourselves. Whether it is the thankfulness of the heart, the praise of the soul or the adoration of the spirit, we long to bestow them on him and in this sense they become our sacrifices of worship.

They are not sacrifices aimed at appeasing an angry God or bribing a reluctant God, but positive acts in which we gladly give something of ours to him. And this calls for more than mere words; there must be substance to the giving over of our lives, just as Abraham visibly and physically gave Isaac to be bound on the altar.

The final vision of ultimate worship in the Scriptures is centred on the Lamb slain before the foundation of the world, a reminder afresh that all worship is for ever joined to sacrifice.

In the meantime, the apostle Paul describes our worship in terms of our surrendered lives: 'I urge you, brothers, in view of God's mercy, to offer your bodies as living sacrifices, holy and pleasing to God—which is your spiritual act of worship' (Romans 12:1). Our worship is only as rich as our life.

Each day provides us with new opportunities to demonstrate our commitment to Christ by laying down our lives for him. Paul's idea of the surrendered life is not to live as a religious recluse, cut off from the world of need, imprisoned in religious thinking. Instead, it is to be the outward flow of the love of God to the world around us.

To touch that world will not require most of us to cross the oceans. It will mean involvement with the immediate world of our own neighbourhood, our street, our office, our home. Here we are provided with a multitude of opportunities to worship God by giving ourselves to serve the needs of others. We can give him our eyes through which to look with compassion, our mouth through which to speak, our hands through which to heal, our feet through which to go, and our hearts through which to love. This is our worship.

This marks the dividing-line between the religious and the spiritual, between the Pharisee and the Samaritan. Jesus was never out of touch. The Christ who daily closed in with his Father in worship was the same Christ who daily walked through crowded streets bringing God to the people.

To live this way ourselves requires the denial of our selfish wants and the giving of ourselves to serve the desires of God.

Worship is more than singing songs and raising our hands in praise to the Almighty. It means giving our money, our time, our counsel, our understanding, our care—our bag of rice.

God will never require us to pay a cost or make a sacrifice greater than the one he has already been willing to make himself. Christ on the cross is the ultimate sacrifice, the ultimate example, the ultimate provocation for all worship. In the light of that, we can identify with C.T. Studd when he said, 'If Jesus Christ be God and died for me, then no sacrifice can be too great for me to make for him.'

Today, people's values have lost direction. Worth is measured in material terms: the house we own, the car we drive, the vacations we take. This root of materialism in the human heart ensures that those who have abundant possessions are never content; there will always be the desire for more. For them, money represents power. It gives them the ability to control others, to manipulate and manoeuvre their way through life, taking advantage of people and situations to further their own ends.

But for the lover of God the material things of this world have lost their power. The cross has effectively severed the root of materialism and the heart is now captured to a higher goal, that of God himself. Our values in life are now different. The thing we long for most is to bring pleasure to the heart of our God.

When everything we are and have has been yielded to him, we no longer fear for ourselves in life. Like Paul we can say, 'I know whom I have believed, and am convinced that he is able to guard what I have entrusted to him for that day' (2 Timothy 1:12).

It leaves us gloriously free in life for we are no longer grasping and greedy, no longer trying to hold on to the material things we have received. They are ours to enjoy and to use to his glory. But whether we have them or not will never alter the fact that, in finding Christ and worshipping him, we have discovered and are enjoying the thing that excites the heart the most because it is engaged in that which is of utmost value.

To have everything without God is to be poor beyond description, but to have God and nothing else is to be rich beyond compare.

When we have seen the worth of God which is the touchstone of worship, then our love can never hold on to anything that we are or have. Everything is immediately his.

> Were the whole realm of nature mine,
> That were an offering far too small;
> Love so amazing, so divine,
> Demands my soul, my life, my all.

22

Worship brings it all into perspective

The serene, silent beauty of a holy life is the most powerful influence in the world, next to the might of God.
Blaise Pascal

National Sales Manager of the year again. This was the third consecutive year. I could understand why. Anybody meeting Joe was immediately impressed by his sense of confidence and affable nature. You never felt he was trying to sell you anything, yet you always wanted to buy from him. You felt he was serving your interests.

Joe was a man's kind of man—strong, decisive, clear as to where he was going. Everything about him spoke of a well-balanced personality, a man whose life had come together well. There seemed to be harmony between the person, his job, his family and life around him.

One day Joe telephoned and asked if he could drop by for an hour to see me. It came as a shock to be told that he and his wife, Susan, were considering breaking up. I had had no hint of a problem. They seemed well suited to each other, pleasant to be with, happy and hospitable.

Susan seemed to be the ideal person for Joe. Bubbling with

happiness, easy-going when surrounded by pressures, she took in her stride last-minute changes to plans. Where other women would go to pieces, Susan seemed to cope without effort. At special functions she would glide confidently around the room, the perfect partner alongside Joe.

'Whatever could be wrong?' I wondered. When, later, they came to see me together, I could see in their eyes the pain they were both feeling. As we sat down I looked at Joe's face intently. It was pale and strained. Susan dabbed at her eyes again and again, wiping away the tears that seemed to be instantly replenished from some hidden spring.

As they shared their hearts it became obvious how deceived I had been. For behind the cool, strong, decisive image he projected, Joe was a man grappling with frustrations about himself. He was plagued with feelings of inadequacy as a husband and a father, labouring under a guilt complex that, whereas he was winning in the national sales league, he was losing inside his home.

He looked woefully at me and whispered, 'I've analysed our marriage and looked hard at where it's all going. The future looks bleak. I'm convinced Susan will be happier without me. I'm not blaming her for anything—I know the problem is in myself.'

After listening for some time, I put before Joe that his use of phrases like 'analysed our situation' and 'the future looks bleak' showed that he was approaching the problems of his marriage in the same way that he approached sales meetings.

'Joe,' I said, 'both of you love God, and each other, and you know that love operates very differently from the rules of marketing.' I suggested that, before going through with the decision to separate, they should wait a week longer, during which time I asked Joe to visit Mary, an elderly lady in the church.

'Joe,' I said, 'without explaining the details to her, ask her to pray with you for your marriage.'

Being the kind of man he was, Joe contacted Mary immediately and the next day went to see her. Within forty-eight hours he was phoning me for another meeting. This time, as he walked through the door, I knew things had changed for him. His face was wreathed in smiles. He was so relaxed that I couldn't help but ask, 'What's happened, Joe?'

'I feel my life has been turned upside down and inside out,' he replied enthusiastically. 'I shared with Mary that I needed prayer for my family and marriage. She listened kindly and then simply said, "Well, Joe, let's wait on the Lord and worship him and see what he might say about it." '

I smiled, because in my mind's eye I could see her. I knew what he was about to say before he said it, because I had had similar experiences with Mary myself.

'She just knelt by her chair,' Joe went on, 'and began to worship the Lord. She seemed to forget about my being in the room. It was the way she praised him, thanked him, loved him—I just felt I'd hardly begun in life. It was so catching that I forgot my reasons for being there and started to worship with her, and soon felt as though I was being washed on the inside. I felt so clean, so loved, so warm, so peaceful. It was as though everything inside me just came together and I knew that what was really wrong inside me was I hadn't given myself to loving God as I ought. So I was unable to love Susan as I should.

'I've often prayed about my wants and needs,' he continued, 'and over recent weeks I've never prayed so much in my life to save my marriage. But I still felt all knotted up inside. Now, instead of asking and pleading, I found myself so in love with God that I wanted to say it to him over and over again.

'I don't know what else to say,' he concluded, 'except that I went home different. And it's been different for Susan and me ever since—we love each other, we're in love with God, we're praising and worshipping together.'

What Joe said that day has been repeated many times in other people's experience. When we move out of our own needs and focus our worship on God's worth, when we love him with all that is in us, it triggers a divine response that takes care of the things that concern us before we even ask him about them. 'Before they call I will answer; while they are still speaking

I will hear' (Isaiah 65:24).

You can't love others as you would desire until you love God as you should. The psalmist discovered it when he said, 'Delight yourself in the Lord and he will give you the desires of your heart' (Psalm 37:4).

Joe, the national sales winner, Joe the company figure, Joe the man of decision, had been touched by the water of life flowing from one of God's hidden people, a woman the source of whose richness of life was to be found in the fact that all her desires centred in Christ.

The bookshelves are lined with books on self-motivation, self-achievement, self-development, how to be a better this, that or the other. But, in the final analysis, nothing influences our world more than those whose lives bear the imprint of Christ. Around them there is an aura of peace. They live contentedly in the will and presence of God amid a world rushing to find greatness and pressing forward to achievement.

I've met them over the years, men and women whose lives are so taken up with love for God that to be in their presence is like being in his. Time with them, drinking from the cup of their counsel and fellowship and joining them in the heart of praise, is a liberating experience.

Theirs is a life of worship, a life that carries the glory of God's presence into the world around. They are enjoying the same experience as Moses: 'When Moses came down from Mount Sinai with the two tablets of the Testimony in his hands, he was not aware that *his face was radiant* because he had spoken with the Lord' (Exodus 34:29).

They are not aware of bearing the presence and glory of God. They would never dream of making such a claim. But we see what they do not—and thank God for such people. To be touched by their lives only intensifies our own thirst and longing for God.

I remember once looking out over a valley, where the early morning haze softened the scene. The rains had recently come, causing the valley to spring to life, covering itself with a lush coat of green grass. There was no rush of cars or noise of snarled traffic—this was not the pollution-choked air of the city but Africa's Rift Valley.

Small spirals of smoke could be seen rising from the Masai kraals. Wildebeest were moving lazily together. I peered intently at the waterhole where the deer were gathering to drink, together with a zebra or two. Other animals, too, would come and go. The varied animals had this one thing in common: they needed to drink.

We, too, constantly yearn to be with him. The psalmist expressed it, 'As the deer pants for streams of water, so my soul pants for you, O God. My soul thirsts for God, for the living God' (Psalm 42:1-2).

Again he cried, 'O God, you are my God, earnestly I seek you; my soul thirsts for you, my body longs for you, in a dry and weary land where there is no water. I have seen you in the sanctuary and beheld your power and your glory' (Psalm 63:1-2).

It is this thirst for God in our spirit that continues to pull us upwards, urging us in worship to come and bow before him who bids us welcome.

As our thirst is thus quenched, as we worship our God, every part of our life comes into peace.